T0020838

THE "I LOVE MY AIR FRYER"

Low-Carb

RECIPE BOOK

From *Carne Asada with Salsa Verde* to *Key Lime Cheesecake*,
175 Easy and Delicious Low-Carb Recipes

Michelle Fagone of CavegirlCuisine.com
Author of *The Everything® Air Fryer Cookbook*

Adams Media
New York London Toronto Sydney New Delhi

To Samantha and Calla
You two have grown up to be such beautiful, strong young women. I couldn't be prouder.
All my love, Mom

Adams Media
An Imprint of Simon & Schuster, Inc.
57 Littlefield Street
Avon, Massachusetts 02322

Copyright © 2020 by Simon & Schuster, Inc.

All rights reserved, including the right to reproduce this book or portions thereof in any form whatsoever. For information address Adams Media Subsidiary Rights Department, 1230 Avenue of the Americas, New York, NY 10020.

First Adams Media trade paperback edition January 2020

ADAMS MEDIA and colophon are trademarks of Simon & Schuster.

For information about special discounts for bulk purchases, please contact Simon & Schuster Special Sales at 1-866-506-1949 or business@simonandschuster.com.

The Simon & Schuster Speakers Bureau can bring authors to your live event. For more information or to book an event contact the Simon & Schuster Speakers Bureau at 1-866-248-3049 or visit our website at www.simonspeakers.com.

Photographs by James Stefiuk

Manufactured in the United States of America

10 9 8 7 6 5 4 3 2

Library of Congress Cataloging-in-Publication Data
Names: Fagone, Michelle, author.
Title: The "I love my air fryer" low-carb recipe book / Michelle Fagone of CavegirlCuisine.com, author of The everything® air fryer cookbook.
Description: Avon, Massachusetts: Adams Media, 2020.
Series: "I love my" series.
Includes index.

Identifiers: LCCN 2019038279 | ISBN 9781507212264 (pb) | ISBN 9781507212271 (ebook)
Subjects: LCSH: Low-carbohydrate diet--Recipes. | Hot air frying. | LCGFT: Cookbooks.
Classification: LCC RM237.73 .F34 2020 | DDC 641.5/6383--dc23
LC record available at https://lccn.loc.gov/2019038279

ISBN 978-1-5072-1226-4
ISBN 978-1-5072-1227-1 (ebook)

Many of the designations used by manufacturers and sellers to distinguish their products are claimed as trademarks. Where those designations appear in this book and Simon & Schuster, Inc., was aware of a trademark claim, the designations have been printed with initial capital letters.

Always follow safety and commonsense cooking protocols while using kitchen utensils, operating ovens and stoves, and handling uncooked food. If children are assisting in the preparation of any recipe, they should always be supervised by an adult.

The information in this book should not be used for diagnosing or treating any health problem. Not all diet and exercise plans suit everyone. You should always consult a trained medical professional before starting a diet, taking any form of medication, or embarking on any fitness or weight training program. The author and publisher disclaim any liability arising directly or indirectly from the use of this book.

Contains material adapted from the following titles published by Adams Media, an Imprint of Simon & Schuster, Inc.: *The Everything® Air Fryer Cookbook* by Michelle Fagone, copyright © 2018, ISBN 978-1-5072-0912-7, and *The Everything® Low-Carb Meal Prep Cookbook* by Lindsay Boyers, CHNC, copyright © 2018, ISBN 978-1-5072-0731-4.

Contents

Introduction

If you have an air fryer, you probably already know that it is a revolutionary appliance that can save you time and help you live a healthier life. New to this amazing device? Well, you'll be excited to learn that you'll soon be using your air fryer to prepare nearly every meal, from breakfast and side dishes to dinner and dessert. What's so special about air frying, you ask?

The air fryer can replace your oven, microwave, deep fryer, and dehydrator *and* cook delicious meals in a fraction of the time you're used to. If you are looking to enjoy healthy meals but don't have a lot of time to spare, the air fryer is a game changer.

An air fryer can also help with your success on a low-carb diet. Typically, fried foods are filled with carbohydrates, so you might assume you have to avoid them altogether. However, with the air fryer, you still get the crunch of your favorite fried recipes—without the carbs. And you can choose your own low-carb breading! Another benefit to air frying is the short cooking times it provides. Long-term success on a low-carb diet is often attributed to ease of preparing healthy, diverse meals. That's why your air fryer will be your best friend throughout your low-carb journey and help you stay on track, even on those days when you are short on time—or patience.

In *The "I Love My Air Fryer" Low-Carb Recipe Book*, you'll learn everything you need to know about using an air fryer, as well as some basics that will help you find success while eating a low-carb diet. You'll also find the perfect recipe for every occasion, from filling breakfasts, like BLT Frittata, to mouthwatering dinners for your whole family, such as Texas Rib Eye Steak—and everything in between. So, let's get air frying!

1

Low-Carb Air Fryer Essentials

The air fryer is one of the most popular kitchen appliances for good reason: Fried food can be made and enjoyed guilt-free! It also cooks foods quicker than your conventional oven, doesn't heat up your living space, and is easy to clean. In this chapter, you will learn more about the functions of the air fryer and its handy accessories. You will also find further information on the low-carb diet, from what it really means to how it can impact your life for the better.

Keep in mind that while this chapter will cover the basics of using an air fryer, the first step is reading the manual that your air fryer came with. All air fryers are different, and there are a lot of different models on the market. Learning the ins and outs of your specific air fryer is the key to success, and it will familiarize you with troubleshooting issues as well as safety functions. Reading over the manual and washing all parts with warm, soapy water before the first use will get you ready to unleash your culinary finesse!

Why Own an Air Fryer?

The air fryer works by baking foods with a constant stream of circulating hot air that cooks food evenly and quickly, crisping up edges as it does its job. This is why the air fryer has quicker cooking times than a conventional oven—but the benefits of this appliance don't stop there. Here are a few more reasons to switch to air frying:

• **It replaces other cooking appliances.** Thanks to its quicker cooking times, the air fryer is the perfect alternative to your oven—but it can also replace your deep fryer, dehydrator, and microwave! In one device, you'll be able to whip up perfect meals, snacks, sides, and more without sacrificing any of the flavor.

• **It uses little to no cooking oil.** Traditionally cooked fried foods are prepared by submerging foods in heated oil, which means they are high in bad fats and calories. Also, when oil is heated beyond its smoking point, as with deep-frying, it can produce toxic fumes and free radicals. The air fryer drastically cuts down on fatty oils, meaning more nutritious meals. This can also lead to weight loss and better overall health.

• **It makes vegetables appeal to the pickiest eaters.** A little low-carb breading and a fresh dipping sauce can turn zucchini into tasty fries. And a little ground pork rind breading on some cod can be the gateway recipe from fish sticks to a simple salmon fillet.

- **It saves your energy bill.** When cooking casseroles or thicker cuts of meat, your traditional oven can provide a heat source that is not always welcomed, especially on those long, hot days. The contained heat of the air fryer will keep your air conditioner from working overtime.

Purchasing an Air Fryer

There are several brands, sizes, and shapes of air fryers available. This book is based on a four-person 1,425-watt air fryer with a 1-pound, 13-ounce capacity. Depending on your chosen model, the size of your food batches will vary, but cooking times will not be affected. For example, if you own a smaller two-person model, simply halve the ingredients in the chosen recipe. As for the temperature range, some air fryers allow you to dehydrate foods because you can cook them at a very low temperature for a long period of time. You'll want to make sure your air fryer has the appropriate cooking capacity and temperature range to meet your needs.

Air Fryer Functions

Settings can vary among different air fryer models on the market. Some of the newer types offer digital settings to control the temperature and time, while others have analog dials as well as preset temperatures for certain fresh and frozen foods. All recipes in this book were created using manual times and temperatures. Every air fryer allows you to set these yourself. Still, it is important to know how the cooking programs work on your air fryer and when to use them. And although some brands will claim you don't need to preheat the air fryer, skipping this step can alter cooking times. The recipes in this book include preheating instructions.

In addition, because the air fryer basket is going to be used when making most of your air-fried foods, finding a model with a quick-release button will make your life easier. This button releases the fryer basket containing food from the bottom basket so you can shake or flip the food with ease.

Air Fryer Accessories

The air fryer comes with a basic fryer basket; however, there are many other recipes that can be made with the purchase of a few accessories. Before you purchase any of these, make sure they work with your size and brand of air fryer. Here are some of the common air fryer accessories:

- **Metal holder.** This round metal rack allows for cooking a second layer of food in the air fryer.

- **Skewer rack.** This is similar to a metal holder but also contains four metal skewers for roasting meat and vegetable shish kebabs.

- **Ramekin.** Small ramekins are great for making mini cakes and quiches. If they're oven safe, they're safe to use in your air fryer.

- **Cake barrel.** You can purchase both round and square versions. A cake barrel is used for desserts, casseroles, and egg dishes. As a bonus, both types of barrel have a handle, making retrieval from the air fryer a cinch.

- **Cupcake pan.** This pan usually comes with seven silicone cupcake liners (also called *baking cups*) that are oven safe and great for mini meatloaves, cupcakes, on-the-go frittatas, quick breads, and muffins. They are reusable and dishwasher safe, making cleanup a snap!

- **Parchment paper.** Specially precut parchment paper makes cleanup even easier when baking with your air fryer. You can also find parchment paper with precut holes for steaming.

- **Pizza pan.** This is a shallow pan that allows you to make mini pizzas, as well as a variety of other recipes, such as biscuits, corn bread, Dutch pancakes, and even the delectable Giant Chocolate Chip Cookie found in Chapter 9!

- **Grill pan.** This replaces the air fryer basket and is used for grilling fish, meat, and vegetables. Because there are no side walls, the pan allows for a bit more room than the air fryer basket.

Accessory Removal

When cooking pot-in-appliance, you'll want to be careful to avoid burning yourself once it's time to remove the inserted dish. Here are a couple useful tools for safely removing items from your air fryer:

- **Tongs.** Wooden or silicone-tipped tongs will help you remove pans that don't have handles, as well as flip food items, such as egg rolls and meat.

- **Oven mitts.** Heat-resistant mini mitts, or pinch mitts, are small food-grade silicone oven mitts that will help you lift pots out of the air fryer. They are more heat-resistant and less cumbersome than traditional oven mitts, which can prove to be bulky in the tight fryer basket.

- **Accessory removal hack.** You can also create an aluminum foil sling to lift a heated dish out of the air fryer. Simply fold a 10″ × 10″ square of aluminum foil in half, then fold again lengthwise. Place the sling underneath the bowl or pan before cooking.

Cleaning and Seasoning Your Air Fryer

After using your air fryer, unplug the appliance and allow it to completely cool. Adding cooler water to your fryer basket can cause warping. Although the removable parts are dishwasher safe, washing them by hand with warm, soapy water can lengthen the life of those coated nonstick parts.

To clean the air fryer pan you'll need to:

1. Remove the air fryer pan from the base. Fill the pan with hot water and dish soap. Let the pan soak with the frying basket inside for 10 minutes.
2. Clean the basket thoroughly with a sponge or brush.
3. Remove the fryer basket and scrub the underside and outside walls.

4. Clean the air fryer pan with a sponge or brush.

5. Let everything air-dry and return to the air fryer base.

6. Wipe the outside of the air fryer base with a damp cloth.

Once dry, the fryer basket can also be seasoned. You may have heard this term with cast-iron pans, but the air fryer basket can benefit from seasoning as well. Preheat the air fryer with the basket for 5 minutes at 400°F. Remove the basket and when cool enough to touch, spread a thin layer of coconut oil on the inside using a paper towel. Then simply heat the basket for an additional 2 minutes. This will help extend the life of the nonstick coating in the basket.

Breaking Down the Low-Carb Diet

Now that you have the basics of cooking with the air fryer down, it's time to take a look at the low-carb diet. What exactly does it mean? What foods are cut out or reduced? What is a net carb? Well, in the simplest terms, a low-carb diet means reducing the amount of carbohydrates you consume. Different low-carb diets have varying guidelines on how many carbohydrates, proteins, and fats you should eat daily, but typically, a low-carb diet macronutrient breakdown looks something like this:

- Less than 20 percent of calories from carbohydrates
- 25–30 percent of calories from protein
- 50–55 percent of calories from fat

Most low-carb diets eliminate the obvious sources of carbohydrates, like sugar, processed foods, and desserts. Others also eliminate or reduce amounts of fruit and starchy vegetables like potatoes. There is no one-size-fits-all low-carb diet; it's up to you to find the balance of macronutrients and food choices that works for your body.

Total Carbs versus Net Carbs

When following a low-carb diet, you'll probably see or hear the term *net carbs*. The concept of net carbs is that certain carbohydrates affect your body in different ways, so you can count them differently when following a low-carb diet.

Refined sugars and starches—or carbohydrates that come from things like potatoes, white bread, and sugar-laden desserts—are absorbed quickly into your bloodstream, causing a rapid spike in blood sugar and insulin and affecting the way your body stores fat. On the other hand, complex carbohydrates—like the fiber from fruits and vegetables—move slowly through the digestive system and have little to no effect on blood sugar and insulin levels. In fact, some carbohydrates like insoluble fiber and sugar alcohols (erythritol and xylitol, to name two) move through the digestive system without entering your blood at all.

Based on this concept, some low-carb diets require you to count net carbohydrates instead of total carbohydrates. To calculate net carbohydrates, you'll simply subtract fiber and sugar alcohols from the total carbohydrate count. For example, if food contains 10 grams of total carbohydrates but 5 of those carbohydrates come from fiber and 1 comes from sugar alcohols, then the net carbs would be 4 grams.

The Benefits of a Low-Carb Diet

There are many reasons to go low-carb! Of course, weight loss is a big one, but low-carb diets offer significant health benefits beyond losing those pesky pounds. Check out the main benefits in the following list. When you understand the mechanisms of how something affects your body positively, you're more likely to stay on track:

• **Weight loss.** Low-carb diets help you shed extra pounds fairly quickly. This includes pounds from both excess water (short-term weight loss) *and* fat (long-term weight loss).

• **Better heart health.** Low-carb diets have been shown to improve all the significant markers for heart disease: low-density lipoprotein (or LDL), high-density lipo-protein (or HDL), triglycerides, and blood pressure.

• **Reduced risk of metabolic syndrome.** Metabolic syndrome is a diagnosis given when a person has at least three of the following conditions at once: high blood pressure, high blood sugar, high levels of visceral fat, and abnormal cholesterol and triglyceride levels. Low-carb diets have been shown to dramatically improve every single marker associated with metabolic syndrome.

• **Better brain function.** Low-carb diets have shown promise for improving brain health and function. In one study, older adults who were considered at risk for developing Alzheimer's disease showed improvement in memory after following a low-carb diet for six weeks.

You've Got This!

You are ready to start air frying your own low-carb dishes, and *The "I Love My Air Fryer" Low-Carb Recipe Book* is here to get you started. Make a meal plan during the weekend, then follow the simple and easy-to-make recipes in this book for a week with far less stress. In most cases, a healthy dinner can take less than thirty minutes. So, have fun and happy eating!

2

Breakfast

Getting out the door on time is hard enough as it is—especially if you are shuffling family around as well. Fitting breakfast, not to mention one that is low-carb (most grab-and-go options out there seem to be carb-filled bars and toaster pastries), into this hectic schedule can seem a bit overwhelming at times. Fortunately, the air fryer is here to save your morning, thanks to its shortened cooking time and the time you'll save by not having to stand over the skillet.

This chapter offers a wide range of delicious, easy-to-make breakfast and brunch recipes for your air fryer, including Spicy Sausage Patties, Egg Cups au Fromage, and Cinnamon Breakfast Bread. And once you get comfortable with some of the basics, you should feel free to be creative and make some of your own morning masterpieces. So let your family wake up with a new appreciation for their soon-to-be-favorite kitchen appliance!

Broiled Grapefruit

Broiling a grapefruit helps bring some of the natural sugar to life, and the seasonings this recipe calls for cut some of that tartness that a raw grapefruit has. Don't forget to section the grapefruit before cooking, as it will help the toppings melt down into the crevices. Also, if you want to add a little flair, serve your grapefruit halves with fresh berries on top.

- **Hands-On Time: 5 minutes**
- **Cook Time: 4 minutes**

Serves 2

1 large grapefruit, cut in half

1 tablespoon granular erythritol

2 teaspoons ground cinnamon

⅛ teaspoon ground ginger

2 teaspoons butter, divided into 2 pats

1 Preheat air fryer at 400°F for 3 minutes.

2 Using a paring knife, cut each grapefruit section away from the inner membrane, keeping the sections remaining in the fruit.

3 In a small bowl, combine erythritol, cinnamon, and ginger. Sprinkle over tops of grapefruit halves. Place 1 pat butter on top of each half.

4 Place grapefruit halves in ungreased air fryer basket and cook 4 minutes.

5 Transfer to a medium serving plate and serve warm.

PER SERVING

CALORIES: 93	FAT: 4g
PROTEIN: 1g	SODIUM: 1mg
FIBER: 3g	CARBOHYDRATES: 22g
NET CARBOHYDRATES: 12g	SUGAR: 12g

Spicy Sausage Patties

If your mornings don't typically include heat, you can simply eliminate the red pepper flakes from this recipe. If you're feeling adventurous, grind your own pork from a pork shoulder to replace the pork sausage.

- **Hands-On Time: 10 minutes**
- **Cook Time: 20 minutes**

Serves 4

12 ounces pork sausage

1 tablespoon peeled and grated yellow onion

1 teaspoon dried thyme

⅛ teaspoon ground cumin

⅛ teaspoon red pepper flakes

¼ teaspoon salt

¼ teaspoon freshly ground black pepper

1 tablespoon water

1 Preheat air fryer at 350°F for 3 minutes.

2 Combine sausage, onion, thyme, cumin, red pepper flakes, salt, and black pepper in a large bowl. Form into eight patties.

3 Pour water into bottom of air fryer to ensure minimum smoke from fat drippings. Place 4 patties in air fryer basket lightly greased with olive oil and cook 5 minutes.

4 Flip patties and cook an additional 5 minutes.

5 Transfer patties to a large serving plate and repeat cooking with remaining sausage patties. Serve warm.

PER SERVING

CALORIES: 182	FAT: 13g
PROTEIN: 16g	SODIUM: 190mg
FIBER: 0g	CARBOHYDRATES: 1g
NET CARBOHYDRATES: 0g	SUGAR: 0g

South-of-the-Border Sausage Balls

A perfect side dish for your breakfast table, these spicy and cheesy sausage balls are full of flavor. Enjoy with your favorite eggs and a bowl of fresh berries to round out the meal.

- **Hands-On Time:** 10 minutes
- **Cook Time:** 12 minutes

Serves 4

- ¼ pound loose chorizo
- ¾ pound ground pork sausage
- 2 tablespoons canned green chiles, including juice
- 1 ounce cream cheese, room temperature
- ¼ cup shredded sharp Cheddar cheese

WHAT IS CHORIZO?

Chorizo is a spicy pork sausage often used in Spanish and Mexican cuisine. Spanish chorizo is traditionally dried and cured, while Mexican chorizo is encased and raw. In this recipe, cut the sausage from the casings, or purchase loose.

1 Preheat air fryer at 400°F for 3 minutes.

2 In a large bowl, combine all ingredients. Form mixture into sixteen 1" balls. Place sausage balls in ungreased air fryer basket.

3 Cook 6 minutes, then shake basket and cook an additional 6 minutes until a meat thermometer ensures an internal temperature of at least 145°F.

4 Transfer to a large serving plate and serve warm.

PER SERVING

CALORIES: 301	**FAT:** 23g
PROTEIN: 21g	**SODIUM:** 388mg
FIBER: 0g	**CARBOHYDRATES:** 1g
NET CARBOHYDRATES: 1g	**SUGAR:** 0g

Air-Fried Hard-"Boiled" Eggs

The air fryer provides a supereasy method for hard-boiling eggs. These Air-Fried Hard-"Boiled" Eggs are a perfect protein and can be enjoyed wholly as a snack, sliced into salads, or transformed into deviled eggs.

- **Hands-On Time: 5 minutes**
- **Cook Time: 15 minutes**

Serves 8

8 large eggs
1 cup ice cubes
2 cups water

1 Preheat air fryer at 250°F for 3 minutes.

2 Add eggs to ungreased air fryer basket. Cook 15 minutes.

3 Add ice and water to a large bowl. Transfer cooked eggs to this water bath immediately to stop cooking process. After 5 minutes, peel eggs and serve.

PER SERVING

CALORIES: 71	FAT: 5g
PROTEIN: 6g	SODIUM: 71mg
FIBER: 0g	CARBOHYDRATES: 0g
NET CARBOHYDRATES: 0g	SUGAR: 0g

Sugar-Free Bacon Strips

Sugar-free bacon is available at many local grocers; however, if you cannot find any in your region, try a specialty grocery store or order online. Also, depending on your bacon preference, adjust cooking times by a minute or two for floppy or crispy bacon.

- **Hands-On Time: 5 minutes**
- **Cook Time: 12 minutes**

Serves 4

2 tablespoons water
8 slices sugar-free bacon, halved

1 Preheat air fryer at 400°F for 3 minutes.

2 Pour water into bottom of air fryer to ensure minimum smoke from fat drippings. Place half of bacon in ungreased air fryer basket and cook 3 minutes. Flip, then cook an additional 3 minutes.

3 Transfer cooked bacon to a medium paper towel–lined serving plate and repeat cooking with remaining bacon. Serve warm.

PER SERVING

CALORIES: 60	FAT: 5g
PROTEIN: 4g	SODIUM: 290mg
FIBER: 0g	CARBOHYDRATES: 0g
NET CARBOHYDRATES: 0g	SUGAR: 0g

Scotch Eggs

Although this treat is traditionally enjoyed as pub food, breakfast is a perfect time of day for it. I mean, c'mon: sausage and eggs—that are portable! If you prefer a runnier yolk, undercook the hard-boiled eggs by a few minutes before preparing the dish.

- **Hands-On Time:** 10 minutes
- **Cook Time:** 14 minutes

Serves 4

1 pound loose pork sausage

2 teaspoons Dijon mustard

2 teaspoons peeled and grated yellow onion

1 tablespoon chopped fresh chives

1 tablespoon chopped fresh parsley

⅛ teaspoon ground nutmeg

½ teaspoon salt

¼ teaspoon freshly ground black pepper

4 large hard-boiled eggs, peeled

1 large egg, beaten

1 cup crushed pork rinds

2 teaspoons olive oil

1 Preheat air fryer at 350°F for 3 minutes.

2 Combine sausage, mustard, onion, chives, parsley, nutmeg, salt, and pepper in a large bowl. Separate mixture into four even balls.

3 Form sausage balls evenly around hard-boiled eggs, then dip in beaten egg and dredge in pork rinds.

4 Place sausage balls in air fryer basket lightly greased with olive oil. Cook 7 minutes, then gently turn and brush lightly with olive oil. Cook an additional 7 minutes.

5 Transfer to a large serving plate and serve warm.

PER SERVING

CALORIES: 402	FAT: 28g
PROTEIN: 34g	SODIUM: 635mg
FIBER: 0g	CARBOHYDRATES: 1g
NET CARBOHYDRATES: 1g	SUGAR: 1g

Bacon Vegetable Morning Hash

To round out this savory breakfast hash, serve it with an egg on top. Poached or over-medium eggs are great, as the runny yolk acts as a sauce for the dish. But if you are in a hurry, just scramble an egg and add it to your bowl. And if you are feeling a little cheesy, throw in some grated Cheddar cheese!

- **Hands-On Time:** 10 minutes
- **Cook Time:** 12 minutes

Serves 4

25 small Brussels sprouts, halved

2 mini sweet peppers, seeded and diced

1 small yellow onion, peeled and diced

3 slices sugar-free bacon, diced

2 tablespoons fresh orange juice

¼ teaspoon salt

1 teaspoon orange zest

1 Preheat air fryer at 350°F for 3 minutes.

2 In a medium bowl, combine all ingredients except orange zest.

3 Add mixture to ungreased air fryer basket. Cook 6 minutes, then toss and cook an additional 6 minutes. Serve warm.

PER SERVING

CALORIES: 86		FAT: 2g	
PROTEIN: 6g		SODIUM: 285mg	
FIBER: 5g		CARBOHYDRATES: 14g	
NET CARBOHYDRATES: 9g		SUGAR: 4g	

MINI SWEET PEPPER SUBSTITUTIONS
Mini sweet peppers have become a staple in many chain grocers; however, if you can't find any, there are several options for substitutes. You can dice a small bell pepper in any preferred color, or, if you're feeling adventurous, use a poblano or jalapeño.

Creamy Herbed Scrambled Eggs

When your scrambled eggs need an extra boost, a little sour cream and goat cheese takes breakfast to the next level. The parsley also adds color and helps brighten the other flavors of the dish.

- **Hands-On Time: 5 minutes**
- **Cook Time: 7 minutes**

Serves 2

4 large eggs
¼ teaspoon salt
⅛ teaspoon freshly ground black pepper
2 teaspoons sour cream
1 tablespoon goat cheese crumbles
1 tablespoon chopped fresh parsley, divided

1 Preheat air fryer at 400°F for 3 minutes.

2 In a small bowl, whisk together eggs, salt, and pepper.

3 Add egg mixture to a cake barrel lightly greased with olive oil. Add barrel to air fryer basket and cook 5 minutes.

4 Remove cake barrel from air fryer and use a silicone spatula to stir eggs. Add sour cream, goat cheese, and half of parsley. Place barrel back in air fryer and cook an additional 2 minutes.

5 Transfer eggs to a medium serving dish and garnish with remaining parsley. Serve warm.

PER SERVING

CALORIES: 167	FAT: 12g
PROTEIN: 14g	SODIUM: 454mg
FIBER: 0g	CARBOHYDRATES: 1g
NET CARBOHYDRATES: 1g	SUGAR: 1g

Maple Sage Breakfast Links

The maple syrup lends a sweetness against the savory spices and the pine-like flavor of the sage. And these links are void of any preservatives and fillers that store-bought counterparts may be filled with.

- **Hands-On Time:** 10 minutes
- **Cook Time:** 9 minutes

Yields 8 sausage links

12 ounces ground mild pork sausage, loose or removed from casings

1 teaspoon rubbed sage

2 tablespoons pure maple syrup

⅛ teaspoon cayenne pepper

¼ teaspoon salt

¼ teaspoon freshly ground black pepper

1 tablespoon water

1 Preheat air fryer at 400°F for 3 minutes.

2 Combine pork, sage, maple syrup, cayenne pepper, salt, and black pepper. Form into eight links.

3 Pour water into bottom of air fryer. Place links in air fryer basket. Cook 9 minutes.

4 Transfer to a plate and serve warm.

PER SERVING (1 SAUSAGE LINK)

CALORIES: 88	FAT: 6g
PROTEIN: 4g	SODIUM: 234mg
FIBER: 0g	CARBOHYDRATES: 4g
NET CARBOHYDRATES: 4g	SUGAR: 3g

Brunchy Shakshuka Bell Pepper Cups

Shakshuka is a Middle Eastern dish that is perfect not only for brunch but also any time of the day. Traditionally, the main ingredients are served in a sauce that contains diced bell peppers, but we've flipped the script in this recipe by putting the ingredients *in* the bell pepper, making each a personal little gift! Use a variety of pepper colors for a more whimsical presentation.

- **Hands-On Time:** 10 minutes
- **Cook Time:** 22 minutes

Serves 4

1 tablespoon olive oil

½ medium yellow onion, peeled and diced

2 cloves garlic, peeled and minced

1 (½") knob turmeric, peeled and minced

1 (14.5-ounce) can diced tomatoes, including juice

1 tablespoon no-sugar-added tomato paste

½ teaspoon smoked paprika

½ teaspoon salt

½ teaspoon granular erythritol

¼ teaspoon ground cumin

¼ teaspoon ground coriander

⅛ teaspoon cayenne pepper

4 small bell peppers, any color, tops removed and seeded

4 large eggs

2 tablespoons feta cheese crumbles

2 tablespoons chopped fresh parsley

1 In a medium saucepan, heat olive oil over medium heat 30 seconds. Add onion and stir-fry 10 minutes until softened.

2 Add garlic and turmeric to pan and heat another minute. Add diced tomatoes, tomato paste, paprika, salt, erythritol, cumin, coriander, and cayenne pepper. Remove from heat and stir.

3 Preheat air fryer at 350°F for 3 minutes.

4 Place bell peppers in ungreased air fryer basket. Divide tomato mixture among bell peppers. Crack one egg onto tomato mixture in each pepper.

5 Cook 9 minutes, then remove from air fryer and sprinkle feta cheese on top of eggs. Place back in air fryer and cook 1 minute.

6 Remove from air fryer and let rest 5 minutes on a large serving plate. Garnish with parsley and serve warm.

PER SERVING

CALORIES: 169	FAT: 10g
PROTEIN: 9g	SODIUM: 519mg
FIBER: 3g	CARBOHYDRATES: 12g
NET CARBOHYDRATES: 8g	SUGAR: 6g

Egg Cups au Fromage

These quick, easy, and portable eggs cups are a riff on the traditional French dish Quiche au Fromage. They have all of the wonderful flavor, with none of the carbs! As a money saver, Swiss cheese can be used instead of Gruyère, thanks to the similar flavor profiles of both cheeses.

- **Hands-On Time:** 10 minutes
- **Cook Time:** 18 minutes

Serves 6

4 large eggs
2 tablespoons heavy cream
⅛ teaspoon salt
⅛ teaspoon freshly ground
    black pepper
⅛ teaspoon ground nutmeg
¼ cup shredded Gruyère
    cheese

1 Preheat air fryer at 350°F for 3 minutes. Lightly grease six silicone muffin cups with olive oil.

2 In a small bowl, whisk together eggs, heavy cream, salt, pepper, and nutmeg. Stir in Gruyère cheese.

3 Distribute egg mixture into prepared muffin cups. Place three cups in air fryer basket and cook 9 minutes.

4 Transfer cooked cups to a large serving plate to cool and repeat cooking with remaining cups. Serve warm.

PER SERVING

CALORIES: 83	FAT: 6g
PROTEIN: 6g	SODIUM: 106mg
FIBER: 0g	CARBOHYDRATES: 0g
NET CARBOHYDRATES: 0g	SUGAR: 0g

Buffalo Chicken Egg Cups

This dish is a great way to utilize any leftover chicken. Plus, because it is cooked in muffin cups, it's a perfect grab-and-go breakfast!

- **Hands-On Time: 10 minutes**
- **Cook Time: 18 minutes**

Serves 6

3 large eggs
2 tablespoons heavy cream
4 teaspoons buffalo wing sauce
¼ cup shredded sharp Cheddar cheese
¼ cup shredded cooked chicken breast

1 Preheat air fryer at 350°F for 3 minutes. Lightly grease six silicone muffin cups with olive oil.

2 In a medium bowl, whisk together eggs, heavy cream, and buffalo wing sauce. Stir in Cheddar cheese and chicken.

3 Distribute egg mixture into prepared muffin cups. Place three cups in air fryer basket and cook 9 minutes.

4 Transfer cooked cups to a large serving plate to cool and repeat cooking with remaining cups. Serve warm.

PER SERVING

CALORIES: 82	FAT: 6g
PROTEIN: 6g	SODIUM: 174mg
FIBER: 0g	CARBOHYDRATES: 1g
NET CARBOHYDRATES: 0g	SUGAR: 0g

Morning Egg Cups

Bacon, cheese, and eggs: the breakfast trifecta! Add a little cream, salt, and pepper, and you have a meal that pleases most everyone. Add diced onion and bell pepper for a sweet crunch.

- **Hands-On Time:** 10 minutes
- **Cook Time:** 18 minutes

Serves 6

3 large eggs
2 tablespoons heavy cream
⅛ teaspoon salt
⅛ teaspoon freshly ground black pepper
3 cooked sugar-free bacon slices, crumbled
¼ cup shredded Cheddar cheese

1 Preheat air fryer at 350°F for 3 minutes. Lightly grease six silicone muffin cups with olive oil.

2 In a small bowl, whisk together eggs, heavy cream, salt, and pepper. Stir in bacon and Cheddar cheese.

3 Distribute egg mixture into prepared muffin cups. Place three cups in air fryer basket and cook 9 minutes.

4 Transfer cooked cups to a large serving plate and repeat cooking with remaining cups. Serve warm.

PER SERVING

CALORIES: 87	**FAT:** 7g
PROTEIN: 5g	**SODIUM:** 189mg
FIBER: 0g	**CARBOHYDRATES:** 0g
NET CARBOHYDRATES: 0g	**SUGAR:** 0g

BLT Frittata

This dish is hearty enough for a brunch and perfect for replenishing your energy after a morning exercise routine. You get all of the flavors of a BLT without the guilt of the grain!

- **Hands-On Time:** 10 minutes
- **Cook Time:** 14 minutes

Serves 2

5 large eggs

¼ teaspoon salt

¼ teaspoon freshly ground black pepper

4 slices cooked sugar-free bacon, crumbled

½ cup grated Cheddar cheese

1 large Roma tomato, cored and sliced

1 cup shredded iceberg lettuce

2 tablespoons sour cream

1 Preheat air fryer at 325°F for 3 minutes.

2 In a medium bowl, whisk together eggs, salt, and pepper. Stir in bacon and Cheddar cheese. Pour mixture into a cake barrel lightly greased with olive oil. Place tomato slices on top.

3 Place barrel in air fryer basket and cook 14 minutes.

4 Transfer cake barrel to a cooling rack to cool 5 minutes, then slice frittata and serve warm topped with lettuce and sour cream.

PER SERVING

CALORIES: 396	FAT: 29g
PROTEIN: 27g	SODIUM: 956mg
FIBER: 1g	CARBOHYDRATES: 6g
NET CARBOHYDRATES: 5g	SUGAR: 4g

Tomato and Spinach Frittata

Serve this light and tasty frittata on one of those lazy weekend mornings. Pour yourself a mimosa, find a series that you've been meaning to watch, and crawl right back under the covers to enjoy your special breakfast in bed.

- **Hands-On Time: 10 minutes**
- **Cook Time: 14 minutes**

Serves 4

5 large eggs

¼ teaspoon salt

¼ teaspoon freshly ground black pepper

½ cup fresh baby spinach leaves

1 large shallot, peeled and diced

4 ounces goat cheese crumbles

1 large Roma tomato, cored and sliced

1 Preheat air fryer at 325°F for 3 minutes.

2 In a medium bowl, whisk together eggs, salt, and pepper. Stir in spinach, shallot, and goat cheese. Pour mixture into a cake barrel lightly greased with olive oil. Place tomato slices on top.

3 Place barrel in air fryer basket and cook 14 minutes.

4 Transfer to a cooling rack to cool 5 minutes in cake barrel, then slice and serve warm.

PER SERVING

CALORIES: 207	FAT: 14g
PROTEIN: 15g	SODIUM: 362mg
FIBER: 1g	CARBOHYDRATES: 4g
NET CARBOHYDRATES: 3g	SUGAR: 2g

Fiesta Breakfast Casserole

Loaded with flavor, this casserole will have your taste buds doing a little dance. Not only is it a tasty breakfast, but it could even be used as a Taco Tuesday meal, with the green chiles and avocado helping make your case. But do you really need an excuse to eat breakfast for dinner?

- **Hands-On Time: 10 minutes**
- **Cook Time: 14 minutes**

Serves 2

5 large eggs

2 tablespoons heavy cream

½ teaspoon ground cumin

¼ teaspoon salt

¼ teaspoon freshly ground black pepper

¼ cup loose cooked spicy breakfast sausage

½ cup queso fresco cheese crumbles

1 large Roma tomato, cored, seeded, and diced

1 (4.5-ounce) can green chiles, including juice

1 small avocado, peeled, pitted and diced

1 Preheat air fryer at 325°F for 3 minutes.

2 In a medium bowl, whisk together eggs, heavy cream, cumin, salt, and pepper. Stir in sausage, queso fresco cheese, tomato, chiles, and avocado. Pour mixture into a cake barrel lightly greased with olive oil.

3 Place barrel in air fryer basket and cook 14 minutes.

4 Transfer barrel to a cooling rack to cool 5 minutes, then slice and serve warm.

PER SERVING

CALORIES: 570	FAT: 44g
PROTEIN: 28g	SODIUM: 1,397mg
FIBER: 9g	CARBOHYDRATES: 18g
NET CARBOHYDRATES: 9g	SUGAR: 5g

Cinnamon Pecan Crunch Cereal

Sometimes low-carb breakfasts can feel a little repetitive with all of the egg dishes when you just want a bowl of cereal. Well, now you can make your own grain-free version! Serve with some unsweetened almond milk or over a bowl of sugar-free yogurt with fresh berries.

- **Hands-On Time: 5 minutes**
- **Cook Time: 6 minutes**

Serves 4

1 cup pecan pieces
1 cup unsalted sunflower seeds
1 cup unsweetened coconut flakes
¼ cup granular erythritol
⅛ cup coconut flour
⅛ cup pecan flour
2 teaspoons ground cinnamon
2 tablespoons melted butter
2 tablespoons raw almond butter
⅛ teaspoon salt

1 Preheat air fryer at 300°F for 3 minutes.

2 Combine all ingredients in a medium bowl.

3 Spoon mixture into an ungreased round 4-cup baking dish. Place in air fryer basket and cook 3 minutes. Stir, then cook an additional 3 minutes.

4 Transfer to an airtight container, let cool 10 minutes, then cover and store at room temperature until ready to serve.

PER SERVING

CALORIES: 646		FAT: 61g	
PROTEIN: 13g		SODIUM: 107mg	
FIBER: 13g		CARBOHYDRATES: 33g	
NET CARBOHYDRATES: 9g		SUGAR: 4g	

WHERE DO I FIND PECAN FLOUR?

Usually, almond flour is the most readily available nut flour on the market, and although sold commercially, nut flours can be a little pricey. But I'll share a secret with you: The only ingredient you need is your choice of nut. Just throw a handful in the food processor and pulse to your desired consistency, whether chunky or fine, depending on the recipe. But don't pulse for too long, as you'll create a nut butter!

Vanilla Nut Granola

Serve this addictive granola as a cereal with your favorite milk, as a trail mix snack, or over Greek yogurt.

- **Hands-On Time: 5 minutes**
- **Cook Time: 6 minutes**

Serves 4

½ cup slivered almonds

½ cup pecan pieces

½ cup unsalted sunflower seeds

½ cup pumpkin seeds

1 cup unsweetened coconut flakes

¼ cup granular erythritol

⅛ cup coconut flour

⅛ cup almond flour

1 teaspoon vanilla extract

2 tablespoons melted butter

2 tablespoons raw almond butter

⅛ teaspoon salt

1 Preheat air fryer at 300°F for 3 minutes.

2 Combine all ingredients in a medium bowl.

3 Spoon mixture into an ungreased round 4-cup oven-safe baking dish and place in air fryer basket. Cook 3 minutes, then stir and cook an additional 3 minutes.

4 Transfer to an airtight container and cool 10 minutes, then cover and store at room temperature until ready to serve.

PER SERVING

CALORIES: 613	FAT: 57g
PROTEIN: 16g	SODIUM: 109mg
FIBER: 11g	CARBOHYDRATES: 31g
NET CARBOHYDRATES: 8g	SUGAR: 4g

Cinnamon Breakfast Bread

If you are missing that good ole stack of pancakes in the morning, this breakfast bread will be your new favorite. Serve topped with butter, sugar-free syrup, fresh berries, or all of the above!

- **Hands-On Time:** 5 minutes
- **Cook Time:** 10 minutes

Serves 2

½ cup finely ground almond flour
¼ cup powdered erythritol
½ teaspoon baking powder
⅛ teaspoon salt
2 tablespoons butter, melted
1 large egg
½ teaspoon unflavored gelatin
½ teaspoon vanilla extract
½ teaspoon ground cinnamon

1 Preheat air fryer at 300°F for 3 minutes.

2 In a medium bowl, combine flour, erythritol, baking powder, and salt. Set aside.

3 In a small bowl, combine butter, egg, gelatin, vanilla, and cinnamon. Add egg mixture to flour mixture and stir until smooth.

4 Spoon mixture into an ungreased pizza pan. Place pan in air fryer basket and cook 10 minutes.

5 Remove pan and let set 5 minutes, then slice and serve warm.

PER SERVING

CALORIES: 305	**FAT:** 28g
PROTEIN: 10g	**SODIUM:** 284mg
FIBER: 3g	**CARBOHYDRATES:** 31g
NET CARBOHYDRATES: 4g	**SUGAR:** 1g

Pecan Streusel Coffee Cake

A sweet bite to enjoy with a cup of coffee or tea, this cake is layered to perfection. A little is all you'll need. It consists of cake and a cinnamon layer topped with a creamy cheesecake and pecan streusel—but don't let the long ingredient list scare you away: A lot of the ingredients are repeated in each layer.

- **Hands-On Time: 5 minutes**
- **Cook Time: 15 minutes**

Serves 8

For Cake
½ cup finely ground almond flour
¼ cup granular erythritol
½ teaspoon baking powder
½ teaspoon instant espresso powder
⅛ teaspoon salt
2 tablespoons butter, melted
1 large egg
½ teaspoon cream of tartar
½ teaspoon vanilla extract
½ teaspoon ground cinnamon

For Cinnamon Layer
3 tablespoons butter, melted
⅓ cup granular erythritol
1 tablespoon ground cinnamon
2 tablespoons cassava flour

For Cheesecake
6 ounces cream cheese, room temperature
2 tablespoons granular erythritol
¼ teaspoon vanilla extract
1 large egg

For Pecan Streusel
⅓ cup pecan pieces
¼ teaspoon ground cinnamon
¼ teaspoon vanilla extract
¼ cup granular erythritol
2 tablespoons butter, melted

1 **To make Cake:** In a medium bowl, combine all ingredients. Spread in a 7" springform pan greased with cooking spray.

2 **To make Cinnamon Layer:** In a small bowl, combine all ingredients. Spread over cake in pan.

3 **To make Cheesecake:** In a medium bowl, combine all ingredients until smooth. Spread over cinnamon layer.

4 **To make Pecan Streusel:** In a small bowl, combine all ingredients. Drop in small crumbles over cheesecake.

5 Preheat air fryer at 300°F for 3 minutes. Cover pan with aluminum foil.

6 Place pan in air fryer basket and cook 10 minutes. Remove foil and cook an additional 5 minutes.

7 Let pan cool 30 minutes uncovered, then cover and refrigerate at least 2 hours, up to overnight. Slice and serve.

PER SERVING

CALORIES: 266		FAT: 25g	
PROTEIN: 5g		SODIUM: 148mg	
FIBER: 2g		CARBOHYDRATES: 29g	
NET CARBOHYDRATES: 5g		SUGAR: 1g	

Pumpkin Nut Muffins

Yes, you can still have muffins on a low-carb diet! When that sweet tooth is calling, this is an excellent recipe for staying true to your low-carb regime.

- **Hands-On Time:** 10 minutes
- **Cook Time:** 7 minutes

Serves 6

½ cup almond flour
½ cup granular erythritol
½ teaspoon baking powder
¼ teaspoon pumpkin pie spice
⅛ teaspoon ground nutmeg
⅛ teaspoon salt
¼ cup pumpkin purée
¼ teaspoon vanilla extract
3 tablespoons butter, melted
2 large eggs
¼ cup crushed walnuts

1 Preheat air fryer at 375°F for 3 minutes.

2 In a large bowl, combine flour, erythritol, baking powder, pumpkin pie spice, nutmeg, and salt. Set aside.

3 In a medium bowl, combine pumpkin purée, vanilla, butter, and eggs. Pour wet ingredients into bowl with dry ingredients and gently combine.

4 Add walnuts to batter. Do not overmix. Spoon batter into six silicone cupcake liners lightly greased with olive oil.

5 Place cupcake liners in air fryer basket and cook 7 minutes.

6 Transfer muffins in silicone liners to a cooling rack to cool 5 minutes, then serve.

PER SERVING

CALORIES: 161		**FAT:** 15g
PROTEIN: 5g		**SODIUM:** 107mg
FIBER: 1g		**CARBOHYDRATES:** 19g
NET CARBOHYDRATES: 2g		**SUGAR:** 1g

Strawberry Basil Muffins

Strawberries and basil are a terrific combination, and even better in the form of this tasty breakfast treat. It's perfect for a warm-weather morning—or any morning, really.

- **Hands-On Time: 10 minutes**
- **Cook Time: 7 minutes**

Serves 6

¼ cup almond flour
¼ cup coconut flour
½ cup granular erythritol
½ teaspoon baking powder
⅛ teaspoon salt
½ cup hulled and finely chopped fresh strawberries
¼ teaspoon vanilla extract
3 tablespoons butter, melted
2 large eggs
1 tablespoon chopped fresh basil

1 Preheat air fryer at 375°F for 3 minutes.

2 In a large bowl, combine almond flour, coconut flour, erythritol, baking powder, and salt. Set aside.

3 In a medium bowl, combine strawberries, vanilla, butter, and eggs. Pour wet ingredients into large bowl with dry ingredients. Gently combine.

4 Add basil to batter. Do not overmix. Spoon batter into six silicone cupcake liners lightly greased with olive oil.

5 Place liners in air fryer basket and cook 7 minutes.

6 Transfer muffins in silicone liners to a cooling rack to cool 5 minutes, then serve.

PER SERVING

CALORIES: 127	FAT: 10g
PROTEIN: 4g	SODIUM: 115mg
FIBER: 2g	CARBOHYDRATES: 21g
NET CARBOHYDRATES: 3g	SUGAR: 1g

3

Appetizers, Snacks, and Sauces

Living within certain diet requirements is never harder than when you are with a group of friends. Chips and dips and deep-fried, breaded everything seem to swarm the tables. But boring plates of unhealthy food don't have to be your fate; bring a healthy, delicious low-carb option to share. Or, better yet, throw your own shindig and show everyone what they've been missing! Tasty appetizers and snacks are a great way to bring a group of people together to enjoy a sports game or tide them over until you serve a meal.

Quick, crispy food air-fried in minutes? Now that's how you throw a party! With amazing appetizers and snacks ranging from Chicken Enchilada Dip and Chipotle Avocado Fries to California Roll Deviled Eggs and Eggplant Parm Sticks—paired with delectable sauces like Low-Carb Honey Mustard—the only problem you'll have incorporating the recipes in this chapter into your next social event will be deciding which ones to make. Your guests won't even know they are eating low-carb recipes!

Chicken Enchilada Dip

Serve this ooey-gooey yumminess with your favorite squash slices, carrot sticks, celery stalks, or whatever produce your heart desires. The crudités just act as vessels to get this goodness to your mouth. Who needs tortilla chips?! Also, if you like cilantro, garnish this dip with a little of this fresh herb (or parsley if you prefer) for a gorgeous presentation and added flavor!

- **Hands-On Time:** 10 minutes
- **Cook Time:** 10 minutes

Serves 6

8 ounces cream cheese, room temperature

¼ cup mayonnaise

¼ cup sour cream

1 cup chopped cooked chicken breast

2 tablespoons peeled and chopped yellow onion

1 (4-ounce) can diced green chiles, including juice

1 medium jalapeño, seeded and minced

1 cup shredded Cheddar cheese, divided

¼ cup cored, seeded, and diced fresh vine-ripe tomatoes

1 Preheat air fryer to 400°F for 3 minutes.

2 In a large bowl, mix cream cheese, mayonnaise, and sour cream until smooth. Add chicken, onion, green chiles, jalapeño, and ½ cup Cheddar cheese.

3 Spoon mixture into an ungreased 6″ oven-safe baking dish. Sprinkle remaining cheese on top.

4 Place dish in air fryer basket. Cook 10 minutes.

5 Garnish cooked dip with diced tomatoes and serve warm.

PER SERVING

CALORIES: 333	FAT: 29g
PROTEIN: 14g	SODIUM: 395mg
FIBER: 1g	CARBOHYDRATES: 5g
NET CARBOHYDRATES: 4g	SUGAR: 2g

Hot Reuben Dip

This recipe takes the traditional Reuben sandwich flavors and combines them into one seriously addicting dip. Serve with your favorite vegetables for dipping.

- **Hands-On Time: 10 minutes**
- **Cook Time: 10 minutes**

Serves 6

8 ounces cream cheese, room temperature

¼ cup mayonnaise

¼ cup sour cream

1 cup chopped deli corned beef

1 cup drained sauerkraut

1 cup shredded Swiss cheese, divided

1 teaspoon caraway seeds

1 Preheat air fryer to 400°F for 3 minutes.

2 In a large bowl, mix cream cheese, mayonnaise, and sour cream until combined. Add corned beef, sauerkraut, ½ cup Swiss cheese, and caraway seeds.

3 Spoon mixture into an ungreased 6" oven-safe baking dish. Sprinkle remaining cheese on top.

4 Place dish in air fryer basket. Cook 10 minutes.

5 Serve warm.

PER SERVING

CALORIES: 320	FAT: 29g
PROTEIN: 13g	SODIUM: 583mg
FIBER: 1g	CARBOHYDRATES: 4g
NET CARBOHYDRATES: 4g	SUGAR: 2g

Baked Garlic Ricotta

This has all of the richness and creaminess of a soufflé but is much more forgiving. Serve with vegetables, alongside your favorite protein, or even as an accompaniment to a charcuterie tray.

- **Hands-On Time:** 10 minutes
- **Cook Time:** 7 minutes

Serves 4

2 cloves peeled Simple Roasted Garlic (see recipe in Chapter 4)

1½ cups ricotta cheese

½ cup grated Parmesan cheese

1 large egg, beaten

1 tablespoon olive oil

1 tablespoon fresh lemon juice

¼ teaspoon salt

¼ teaspoon freshly ground black pepper

1 teaspoon finely chopped fresh rosemary

1 Preheat air fryer to 350°F for 3 minutes.

2 Squeeze garlic into a medium bowl. Using the back of a fork, mash until a garlic paste is formed. Add remaining ingredients and combine.

3 Spoon mixture into an ungreased 6″ oven-safe baking dish.

4 Place dish in air fryer basket. Cook 7 minutes.

5 Serve warm.

PER SERVING

CALORIES: 257	FAT: 16g
PROTEIN: 16g	SODIUM: 411mg
FIBER: 0g	CARBOHYDRATES: 5g
NET CARBOHYDRATES: 5g	SUGAR: 1g

Mediterranean Jalapeño Poppers

Kalamata olives + feta cheese + mint leaves = a traditional, tasty combination. Add a little pork and stuff it into jalapeño halves and you've just taken this bar food up a notch! And if you prefer more heat, instead of discarding the jalapeño seeds, simply fold them into the cheese mixture.

- **Hands-On Time:** 10 minutes
- **Cook Time:** 18 minutes

Serves 6

1 tablespoon olive oil
¼ pound ground pork
2 tablespoons pitted and finely diced kalamata olives
2 tablespoons feta cheese
1 ounce cream cheese, room temperature
½ teaspoon dried mint leaves
6 large jalapeños, sliced in half lengthwise and seeded

1 In a medium skillet, heat olive oil over medium-high heat 30 seconds. Add pork and cook 6 minutes until no longer pink. Drain fat.

2 Preheat air fryer to 350°F for 3 minutes.

3 In a medium bowl, combine cooked pork, olives, feta cheese, cream cheese, and mint leaves.

4 Press pork mixture into peppers.

5 Place half of poppers in ungreased air fryer basket. Cook 6 minutes. Transfer to a medium serving plate and repeat cooking with remaining poppers.

6 Serve warm.

PER SERVING

CALORIES: 116	FAT: 10g
PROTEIN: 6g	SODIUM: 125mg
FIBER: 0g	CARBOHYDRATES: 2g
NET CARBOHYDRATES: 1g	SUGAR: 1g

Baked Brie with Orange Marmalade and Spiced Walnuts

Whether you are entertaining your wine group or workout buddies or just lunchin' with your besties, this elegant appetizer will please all. Serve with vegetables—or even a mix of vegetables and crackers for your carb-loving guests. Just be sure to send those leftover crackers home with someone else so you aren't tempted later!

- **Hands-On Time:** 10 minutes
- **Cook Time:** 22 minutes

Serves 6

1 cup walnuts
1 large egg white, beaten
⅛ teaspoon ground cumin
⅛ teaspoon cayenne pepper
1 teaspoon ground cinnamon
¼ teaspoon powdered erythritol
1 (8-ounce) round Brie
2 tablespoons sugar-free orange marmalade

1 Preheat air fryer at 325°F for 3 minutes.

2 Combine walnuts with egg white in a small bowl. Set aside.

3 In a separate small bowl, combine cumin, cayenne pepper, cinnamon, and erythritol. Add walnuts, drained of excess egg white, and toss.

4 Place walnuts in ungreased air fryer basket. Cook 6 minutes, then toss nuts and cook an additional 6 minutes.

5 Transfer to a small bowl and let cool about 5 minutes until easy to handle. When cooled, chop into smaller bits.

6 Adjust air fryer temperature to 400°F. Place Brie in an ungreased pizza pan or on a piece of parchment paper cut to size of air fryer basket. Cook 10 minutes.

7 Transfer Brie to a medium serving plate and garnish with orange marmalade and spiced walnuts.

PER SERVING

CALORIES: 279	FAT: 24g
PROTEIN: 12g	SODIUM: 250mg
FIBER: 2g	CARBOHYDRATES: 8g
NET CARBOHYDRATES: 2g	SUGAR: 1g

Pepperoni Pizza Bread

This snack is after-school perfection! There is no need to heat up those nutrient-lacking frozen pizza rolls when you can make this easy-peasy Pepperoni Pizza Bread instead. Slice into strips and dip in a warmed marinara sauce.

- **Hands-On Time:** 5 minutes
- **Cook Time:** 20 minutes

Serves 4

2 large eggs, beaten
2 tablespoons coconut flour
2 tablespoons cassava flour
⅓ cup whipping cream
¼ cup chopped pepperoni
⅓ cup grated mozzarella cheese
2 teaspoons Italian seasoning
½ teaspoon baking powder
⅛ teaspoon salt
2 tablespoons grated Parmesan cheese
½ cup no-sugar-added marinara sauce, warmed

1 Preheat air fryer at 300°F for 3 minutes.

2 In a medium bowl, combine eggs with coconut flour, cassava flour, whipping cream, pepperoni, mozzarella cheese, Italian seasoning, baking powder, and salt.

3 Pour batter into an ungreased pizza pan.

4 Place pan in air fryer basket and cook 19 minutes. Sprinkle Parmesan cheese on top and cook an additional minute.

5 Remove pan from basket and let set 5 minutes, then slice and serve with warmed marinara sauce.

PER SERVING

CALORIES: 226	FAT: 17g
PROTEIN: 10g	SODIUM: 563mg
FIBER: 2g	CARBOHYDRATES: 10g
NET CARBOHYDRATES: 7g	SUGAR: 3g

Chipotle Avocado Fries

This will become your new addictive, fantastically awesome snack. The air fryer crisps up the outside evenly, and the avocado becomes almost creamy when heated. The soothing nature of the avocado pairs nicely with the heat from the chipotle, but if spice isn't your thing, swap the chipotle powder for some milder smoked paprika.

- **Hands-On Time:** 10 minutes
- **Cook Time:** 10 minutes

Serves 2

1 large egg, beaten

¼ cup almond flour

2 tablespoons ground flaxseed

¼ teaspoon chipotle powder

¼ teaspoon salt

1 large avocado, peeled, pitted, and sliced into 8 "fries"

DOES FLAXSEED NEED TO BE GROUND?

Whole flaxseed that has not been ground often ends up going through your digestive system in its whole form. This is fine; however, in this form your body does not reap the health benefits that can be achieved with ground flaxseed.

1 Preheat air fryer to 375°F for 3 minutes.

2 Place egg in a small dish. Combine almond flour, flaxseed, chipotle powder, and salt in a separate shallow dish.

3 Dip avocado slices into egg. Dredge through flour mixture to coat. Place half of slices in air fryer basket lightly greased with olive oil.

4 Cook 5 minutes. Transfer to a medium serving plate and repeat cooking with remaining avocado slices.

5 Serve warm.

PER SERVING

CALORIES: 334		FAT: 29g	
PROTEIN: 10g		SODIUM: 351mg	
FIBER: 11g		CARBOHYDRATES: 15g	
NET CARBOHYDRATES: 4g		SUGAR: 1g	

Mozzarella Sticklets

This is a mini version of those deep-fried delights found on many appetizer menus—minus the oil. Serve these mini sticks with toothpicks and a warm marinara sauce.

- **Hands-On Time:** 15 minutes
- **Cook Time:** 10 minutes

Serves 6

2 tablespoons all-purpose flour
1 large egg
1 tablespoon whole milk
½ cup plain bread crumbs
¼ teaspoon salt
¼ teaspoon Italian seasoning
10 mozzarella sticks, each cut into thirds
2 teaspoons olive oil

1 In a small bowl, add flour.

2 In another small bowl, whisk together egg and milk.

3 Combine bread crumbs, salt, and Italian seasoning in a shallow dish.

4 Roll a mozzarella sticklet in flour, then dredge in egg mixture, and then roll in bread crumb mixture. Shake off excess between each step. Set aside on a plate and repeat with remaining mozzarella. Place in freezer 10 minutes.

5 Preheat air fryer at 400°F for 3 minutes.

6 Place half of mozzarella sticklets in fryer basket. Cook 2 minutes. Shake. Lightly brush with olive oil. Cook an additional 2 minutes. Shake. Cook an additional 1 minute. Transfer to a serving dish.

7 Repeat with remaining sticklets and serve warm.

PER SERVING

CALORIES: 197	FAT: 12g
PROTEIN: 13g	SODIUM: 471mg
FIBER: 0g	CARBOHYDRATES: 9g
NET CARBOHYDRATES: 9g	SUGAR: 1g

Five Spice Crunchy Edamame

Crispy on the outside and slightly tender on the inside, these snackable bites deliver a healthy dose of fiber, vitamins, and minerals.

- **Hands-On Time: 5 minutes**
- **Cook Time: 16 minutes**

Serves 4

1 cup ready-to-eat edamame, shelled
1 tablespoon sesame oil
1 teaspoon five spice powder
½ teaspoon salt

1 Preheat air fryer at 350°F for 3 minutes.

2 In a small bowl, toss edamame in sesame oil. Place in air fryer basket and cook 5 minutes. Shake. Cook an additional 5 minutes. Shake. Cook an additional 6 minutes.

3 Transfer to a small bowl and toss with five spice powder and salt. Let cool and serve.

PER SERVING

CALORIES: 62	FAT: 5g
PROTEIN: 3g	SODIUM: 292mg
FIBER: 1g	CARBOHYDRATES: 2g
NET CARBOHYDRATES: 1g	SUGAR: 1g

Spicy Sunflower Seeds

Sunflower seeds are a protein powerhouse filled with vitamins and minerals. Crisp them up with a little heat in your air fryer for a lovely treat.

- **Hands-On Time: 10 minutes**
- **Cook Time: 10 minutes**

Serves 4

2 cups unsalted sunflower seeds
2 teaspoons olive oil
2 teaspoons chili garlic paste
¼ teaspoon salt
1 teaspoon granular erythritol

1 Preheat air fryer at 325°F for 3 minutes.

2 Combine all ingredients in a medium bowl until seeds are well coated.

3 Place seeds in ungreased air fryer basket. Cook 5 minutes. Shake basket. Cook an additional 5 minutes.

4 Transfer to a medium serving bowl and serve.

PER SERVING

CALORIES: 397	FAT: 34g
PROTEIN: 13g	SODIUM: 157mg
FIBER: 7g	CARBOHYDRATES: 17g
NET CARBOHYDRATES: 9g	SUGAR: 2g

Roasted Jack-O'-Lantern Seeds

After getting down and dirty with pumpkin guts while carving your jack-o'-lantern, don't forget to save those little gems in the middle of the gunk. The air fryer roasts those seeds for crunchy snacking, so you can enjoy low-carb, antioxidant-rich bites for the rest of the week! And by the way, if you can't get all of the pumpkin guts off of the seeds, don't sweat it: They are edible and add a little extra flavor!

- **Hands-On Time:** 10 minutes
- **Cook Time:** 13 minutes

Serves 4

2 cups fresh pumpkin seeds
1 tablespoon butter, melted
1 teaspoon salt, divided
½ teaspoon onion powder
½ teaspoon dried parsley
½ teaspoon garlic powder
½ teaspoon dried dill
¼ teaspoon dried chives
¼ teaspoon dry mustard
¼ teaspoon celery seed
¼ teaspoon freshly ground
    black pepper

1. Preheat air fryer at 325°F for 3 minutes.

2. In a medium bowl, toss seeds with butter and ½ teaspoon salt.

3. Place seed mixture in ungreased air fryer basket and cook 7 minutes. Using a spatula, turn seeds, then cook an additional 6 minutes.

4. Transfer to a medium serving bowl. Toss with remaining ingredients. Serve.

PER SERVING

CALORIES: 389	FAT: 29g
PROTEIN: 22g	SODIUM: 583mg
FIBER: 4g	CARBOHYDRATES: 9g
NET CARBOHYDRATES: 4g	SUGAR: 0g

Greek Deviled Eggs

Deviled eggs hearken back to the days when bell-bottoms and disco were all the rage. But has this delicious egg treat really ever gone out of fashion? Embrace fusion and try this new take on a classic.

- **Hands-On Time:** 5 minutes
- **Cook Time:** 15 minutes

Serves 4

4 large eggs
1 cup ice cubes
1 cup water
2 tablespoons plain Greek yogurt
2 tablespoons pitted and finely chopped kalamata olives
2 tablespoons goat cheese crumbles
⅛ teaspoon salt
⅛ teaspoon freshly ground black pepper
2 tablespoons finely chopped fresh mint

1 Preheat air fryer at 250°F for 3 minutes.

2 Place eggs in silicone muffin cups to avoid bumping around and cracking during cooking process. Add silicone cups to air fryer basket. Cook 15 minutes.

3 Add ice and water to a medium bowl. Transfer eggs to water bath immediately to stop cooking process. After 5 minutes, carefully peel eggs.

4 Cut eggs in half lengthwise. Spoon yolks into a separate medium bowl. Arrange white halves on a large plate.

5 Using a fork, blend egg yolks with yogurt, olives, goat cheese, salt, and pepper. Spoon mixture into white halves. Garnish with mint and serve.

PER SERVING

CALORIES: 109	FAT: 8g
PROTEIN: 8g	SODIUM: 290mg
FIBER: 0g	CARBOHYDRATES: 1g
NET CARBOHYDRATES: 1g	SUGAR: 1g

WHY CUT THE EGGS LENGTHWISE?

Not only can you turn the deviled egg ingredient list on its head, but you can also try cutting the egg at its width instead of lengthwise. The white part of the egg is more distributed with the yolk filling instead of having one great bite and then one bite with mostly egg whites. Cutting the egg in this different fashion yields a more balanced bite each time.

California Roll Deviled Eggs

If you love the flavors of sushi but rolling your own seems daunting, try this completely accessible take on a sushi roll classic!

- **Hands-On Time:** 5 minutes
- **Cook Time:** 15 minutes

Serves 4

4 large eggs
1 cup ice cubes
1 cup water
2 tablespoons mayonnaise
½ teaspoon coconut aminos
¼ medium ripe avocado, peeled, pitted, and diced
¼ teaspoon wasabi powder
2 tablespoons diced cucumber
¼ cup lump crabmeat, shells discarded
1 sheet nori, sliced
8 slices jarred pickled ginger
1 teaspoon toasted sesame seeds

1 Preheat air fryer at 250°F for 3 minutes.

2 Place eggs in silicone muffin cups to avoid bumping around and cracking during cooking process. Add silicone cups to air fryer basket. Cook 15 minutes.

3 Add ice and water to a medium bowl. Transfer eggs to water bath immediately to stop cooking process. After 5 minutes, carefully peel eggs.

4 Cut eggs in half lengthwise. Spoon yolks into a medium bowl. Arrange white halves on a large plate.

5 Using a fork, blend egg yolks, mayonnaise, coconut aminos, avocado, and wasabi powder until smooth. Mix in diced cucumber. Spoon into white halves.

6 Garnish eggs with crabmeat, nori, and pickled ginger. Sprinkle with sesame seeds and serve.

PER SERVING

CALORIES: 155	FAT: 12g
PROTEIN: 8g	SODIUM: 293mg
FIBER: 2g	CARBOHYDRATES: 3g
NET CARBOHYDRATES: 1g	SUGAR: 0g

Barbecue Turnip Chips

Slicing the turnips paper-thin and consistently is the key to perfect turnip chips. The air fryer will brown the edges, but keep checking them toward the end of the cooking time, as they can go from brown to burned quickly!

- **Hands-On Time:** 10 minutes
- **Cook Time:** 24 minutes

Serves 2

½ teaspoon smoked paprika

¼ teaspoon chili powder

¼ teaspoon garlic powder

⅛ teaspoon onion powder

⅛ teaspoon cayenne pepper

⅛ teaspoon granular erythritol

1 teaspoon salt, divided

1 large turnip, sliced into ⅛"-thick circles

2 teaspoons olive oil

1 Preheat air fryer to 400°F for 3 minutes.

2 In a small bowl, combine paprika, chili powder, garlic powder, onion powder, cayenne pepper, erythritol, and ½ teaspoon salt. Set aside.

3 In a medium bowl, toss turnip slices with olive oil and ½ teaspoon salt.

4 Place half of turnip slices in air fryer basket lightly greased with olive oil and cook 6 minutes. Shake basket and cook an additional 6 minutes.

5 Transfer chips to a medium bowl and repeat cooking with remaining turnip slices. Toss with seasoning mix. Let rest 15 minutes, then serve.

PER SERVING

CALORIES: 71	FAT: 5g
PROTEIN: 1g	SODIUM: 1,235mg
FIBER: 2g	CARBOHYDRATES: 7g
NET CARBOHYDRATES: 5g	SUGAR: 4g

Pimiento Cheese Jalapeño Poppers

This classic Southern spread of cheese, mayonnaise, and pimientos is traditionally served in a sandwich or with crackers, but it makes the perfect filling for spicy jalapeño boats. Because the peppers are seeded, most of the heat is removed. If you like things spicy, though, mix the seeds in with the pimiento cheese to kick it up a notch!

- **Hands-On Time:** 10 minutes
- **Cook Time:** 8 minutes

Yields 10 poppers

½ cup pimiento cheese
5 medium jalapeños, halved lengthwise and seeded

HOW TO MAKE PIMIENTO CHEESE

Although prepared pimiento cheese can be purchased in the deli section of most grocery stores, making it couldn't be any easier! Just combine 16 ounces finely shredded Cheddar cheese with 1 (4-ounce) jar pimientos including juice, ½ cup mayonnaise, ¼ teaspoon salt, and ¼ teaspoon freshly ground black pepper. Refrigerate covered until ready to use.

1 Preheat air fryer at 350°F for 3 minutes.

2 Press pimiento cheese into each jalapeño half.

3 Lay stuffed peppers in ungreased air fryer basket. Cook 8 minutes.

4 Transfer to a large serving plate and serve warm.

PER SERVING (1 POPPER)

CALORIES: 38	FAT: 3g
PROTEIN: 1g	SODIUM: 144mg
FIBER: 0g	CARBOHYDRATES: 2g
NET CARBOHYDRATES: 2g	SUGAR: 0g

Salsa Verde

This classic is obviously great on Mexican taco-style dishes, but don't discount it from your morning egg dishes either! It is fresh, a little spicy, and so easy to make!

- **Hands-On Time:** 10 minutes
- **Cook Time:** 10 minutes

Yields 1½ cups

- ¾ pounds fresh tomatillos, husked
- 1 large jalapeño, stem removed
- 1 bunch (approximately 8) scallions, both ends trimmed
- 3 cloves garlic, peeled
- ½ teaspoon salt
- 1 tablespoon fresh lime juice
- ¼ cup fresh cilantro leaves

1 Preheat air fryer at 400°F for 3 minutes.

2 Place tomatillos and jalapeño in ungreased air fryer basket. Cook 5 minutes.

3 Add scallions and garlic to basket. Cook an additional 5 minutes.

4 Add tomatillos, jalapeño, scallions, and garlic to a food processor or blender. Add remaining ingredients. Pulse or blend until ingredients are finely chopped.

5 Pour into a small sealable container and refrigerate until ready to use, up to five days.

PER SERVING (¼ CUP)

CALORIES: 32	FAT: 1g
PROTEIN: 1g	SODIUM: 200mg
FIBER: 2g	CARBOHYDRATES: 7g
NET CARBOHYDRATES: 5g	SUGAR: 3g

WHAT IS A TOMATILLO?

This nightshade looks like a mini green tomato with a husk. Tomatillos are denser and less sweet than a tomato, with a touch of sourness. Actually berries, these firm little fruits lend a hand in creating a beautiful sauce that can be used in Mexican dishes, on eggs, or spooned across a nice grilled chicken breast.

Jalapeño Popper Tots

These are so tasty! The flavors meld together, and the air fryer crisps these bites up to perfection. And you'll never even know the carb-filled potatoes are missing.

- **Hands-On Time:** 10 minutes
- **Cook Time:** 18 minutes

Serves 4

¾ cup riced cauliflower

2 medium jalapeños, seeded and minced

1 large egg

⅓ cup grated sharp Cheddar cheese

1 ounce cream cheese, room temperature

1 tablespoon peeled and grated yellow onion

⅓ cup almond flour

½ teaspoon salt

¼ teaspoon garlic powder

1 Preheat air fryer at 375°F for 3 minutes.

2 In a medium bowl, combine all ingredients. Form into twelve rectangular mounds (about 1 tablespoon each).

3 Cut a piece of parchment paper to fit bottom of air fryer basket. Place six pieces on parchment paper in basket. Cook 9 minutes. Transfer to a medium serving plate and repeat cooking with remaining pieces.

4 Let rest 5 minutes, then serve warm.

PER SERVING

CALORIES: 143	FAT: 12g
PROTEIN: 7g	SODIUM: 403mg
FIBER: 2g	CARBOHYDRATES: 5g
NET CARBOHYDRATES: 3g	SUGAR: 1g

Cauliflower Pizza Crusts

There are so many options becoming available in the produce section of grocery stores these days. You can also find broccoli rice—and even a cauli-brocco mixture called *confetti rice*. Get creative and try these in the following recipe. You may finally be able to get those picky eaters to eat their vegetables! To make your pizza, top the crust with your favorite toppings and cook in the air fryer for 3 minutes at 400°F.

- **Hands-On Time: 10 minutes**
- **Cook Time: 24 minutes**

Serves 2

1 cup cauliflower rice
1 large egg
½ cup grated mozzarella cheese
1 tablespoon grated Parmesan cheese
1 clove garlic, peeled and minced
1 teaspoon Italian seasoning
⅛ teaspoon salt

1 Preheat air fryer at 400°F for 3 minutes.

2 In a medium bowl, combine all ingredients. Divide mixture in half and spread into two pizza pans greased with cooking spray.

3 Place one pizza pan in air fryer basket and cook 12 minutes. Remove pan from basket and repeat cooking with second pan.

PER SERVING

CALORIES: 112		FAT: 6g	
PROTEIN: 10g		SODIUM: 357mg	
FIBER: 1g		CARBOHYDRATES: 4g	
NET CARBOHYDRATES: 3g		SUGAR: 1g	

CAULIFLOWER RICE
Although premade cauliflower rice can be purchased in most produce or frozen food sections, cauliflower rice is actually very easy to make. The easiest way is to simply grate one head of cauliflower on a box grater. You can also place florets in a blender with 1 cup of water and blend until desired consistency. Then simply strain out the water and pat dry with paper towels.

Bone Marrow Butter

When bone marrow is cooked, it becomes rich and smooth like butter. So, imagine adding it to actual butter: It is a combination that is beyond delicious. Once your steak is off the grill, cut off a slice of this butter and let it melt atop the meat. Or, if you are cooking your beef on the stove, cook it in a little Bone Marrow Butter. Either way, it is sinfully good!

- **Hands-On Time:** 10 minutes
- **Cook Time:** 12 minutes

Serves 4

2 pounds beef bone marrow bones, cut into 2″ sections

2 cloves garlic, peeled and quartered

5 tablespoons butter, softened

1 tablespoon chopped fresh thyme leaves

¼ teaspoon salt

THE DIFFERENCE BETWEEN BONE MARROW BONES AND SOUP BONES

Both bones have marrow, but bone marrow bones are generally cut into 2″ sections with a visible view of the marrow tunnel, making it easier to cook and retrieve the marrow for butter. Soup bones tend to be longer, sometimes with more meat attached, and are more suited for beef bone broth.

1 Soak bones in water in a large bowl and refrigerate 1 hour.

2 Preheat air fryer at 400°F for 3 minutes.

3 Place bones in ungreased air fryer basket. Cook 12 minutes.

4 Remove from basket and let cool 10 minutes, then push marrow out of bones with a small knife or chopstick. Add to a food processor with remaining ingredients and pulse until smooth.

5 Place mixture on a piece of plastic wrap. Fold sides in to create a log. Spin ends until log is tight. Refrigerate 1 hour until firm.

PER SERVING

CALORIES: 214	**FAT:** 23g
PROTEIN: 1g	**SODIUM:** 148mg
FIBER: 0g	**CARBOHYDRATES:** 1g
NET CARBOHYDRATES: 1g	**SUGAR:** 0g

Eggplant Parm Sticks

There are many types of eggplant, so try them all! Any would make a perfect base for this easy low-carb recipe. And don't worry about peeling them, especially the younger ones: The skin is thin and edible.

- **Hands-On Time:** 10 minutes
- **Cook Time:** 24 minutes

Serves 4

2 large eggs

2 tablespoons heavy cream

½ cup crushed pork rinds

½ cup grated Parmesan cheese

½ teaspoon salt

1 medium eggplant, cut into ½" rounds, then sliced into sticks

½ cup no-sugar-added marinara sauce, warmed

1 Preheat air fryer to 400°F for 3 minutes.

2 Whisk together eggs and heavy cream in a medium bowl. In a separate shallow dish, combine pork rinds, Parmesan cheese, and salt.

3 Dip eggplant sticks in egg mixture. Dredge in pork rind mixture. Place half of the eggplant sticks in air fryer basket lightly greased with olive oil.

4 Cook 6 minutes, then flip and cook an additional 6 minutes. Repeat with remaining eggplant sticks.

5 Transfer to a large serving plate and serve with warmed marinara sauce for dipping.

PER SERVING

CALORIES: 166	FAT: 10g
PROTEIN: 11g	SODIUM: 631mg
FIBER: 4g	CARBOHYDRATES: 10g
NET CARBOHYDRATES: 6g	SUGAR: 6g

Low-Carb Honey Mustard

This sauce is an American classic, so it seems only fitting to pay homage to this mixture that can be used in so many ways, especially with air-fried vegetables or as a dressing for salads.

- **Hands-On Time:** 10 minutes
- **Cook Time:** 0 minutes

Yields ¾ cup

¼ cup mayonnaise

2 tablespoons yellow mustard

1 teaspoon Dijon mustard

¼ teaspoon apple cider vinegar

1 tablespoon granular erythritol

Combine all ingredients in a small bowl. Refrigerate covered up to five days until ready to use.

PER SERVING (1 TEASPOON)

CALORIES: 12	FAT: 1g
PROTEIN: 0g	SODIUM: 25mg
FIBER: 0g	CARBOHYDRATES: 0g
NET CARBOHYDRATES: 0g	SUGAR: 0g

Side Dishes

Eating a low-carb diet can seem daunting and boring—sometimes all in the same breath. Often, you tend to concentrate on the protein and don't take the time to fill your plate and body with any healthy sides. All the while, the fresh produce you carefully chose at the store or farmers' market takes a back seat in the refrigerator, eventually getting slimy, until you inevitably toss it out. Not only is it a waste of healthful food, but it is also a big waste of money. Luckily, the air fryer is here to save the day (and your meal). With the air fryer, you can have roasted, seasonal vegetables in minutes while the main dish is being prepared!

In this chapter, you'll find a range of easy, delicious, and surprisingly low-carb side dishes. With recipes from Prosciutto-Wrapped Asparagus and Roasted Radishes, to Citrus Scallions and Broccoli Tots, you will be happy you took those few extra moments to pop a side dish in the fryer. And your body and taste buds will thank you too!

Dilly Dinner Muffins

Sometimes when eating a low-carb diet, you just want a piece of bread. Try these Dilly Dinner Muffins! The dill pairs nicely with the protein in a salmon fillet or grilled chicken, and the mouthfeel of eating bread again will satisfy that craving—without sabotaging your diet.

- **Hands-On Time:** 10 minutes
- **Cook Time:** 12 minutes

Serves 4

1 cup almond flour
1 teaspoon dried dill
⅛ teaspoon salt
¼ teaspoon onion powder
2 teaspoons baking powder
1 large egg
¼ cup plain Greek yogurt
¼ cup grated Parmesan cheese

1 Preheat air fryer at 350°F for 3 minutes.

2 In a medium bowl, combine almond flour, dill, salt, onion powder, and baking powder. Set aside.

3 In a separate small bowl, whisk together egg, yogurt, and Parmesan cheese. Add wet ingredients to dry ingredients and combine until blended.

4 Transfer batter to six silicone muffin cups lightly greased with olive oil. Place muffin cups in air fryer basket and cook 12 minutes.

5 Serve warm.

PER SERVING

CALORIES: 216	FAT: 17g
PROTEIN: 11g	SODIUM: 372mg
FIBER: 3g	CARBOHYDRATES: 8g
NET CARBOHYDRATES: 5g	SUGAR: 2g

Hot Dog Bread

This bread is just fun. It gives you that pigs-in-a-blanket feel without any of the carb-laden guilt. And don't forget to buy some mustard or no-sugar-added ketchup, or make some ketchup at home, to dip this in for the full experience!

- **Hands-On Time: 5 minutes**
- **Cook Time: 10 minutes**

Serves 4

½ cup finely ground almond flour

¼ cup arrowroot flour

1 tablespoon granular erythritol

½ teaspoon baking powder

¼ teaspoon salt

2 tablespoons butter, melted

1 tablespoon no-sugar-added tomato paste

1 large egg

½ teaspoon unflavored gelatin

1 teaspoon dried thyme

2 beef hot dogs, cut into ½" sections

1 Preheat air fryer at 300°F for 3 minutes.

2 In a large bowl, combine flours, erythritol, baking powder, and salt. Set aside.

3 In a small bowl, combine butter, tomato paste, egg, gelatin, and thyme. Add butter mixture to flour mixture and stir until smooth. Fold in hot dogs.

4 Spoon mixture into an ungreased pizza pan. Place pan in air fryer basket and cook 10 minutes.

5 Remove from basket and let set 5 minutes, then slice and serve warm.

PER SERVING

CALORIES: 258	FAT: 21g
PROTEIN: 8g	SODIUM: 427mg
FIBER: 2g	CARBOHYDRATES: 14g
NET CARBOHYDRATES: 9g	SUGAR: 1g

Roasted Radishes

Try this dish next to a juicy steak to take the place of a traditional potato side. The garlic and butter transform the meaty-textured radish into a fantastic recipe—without the guilt of a high carb count.

- **Hands-On Time: 10 minutes**
- **Cook Time: 10 minutes**

Serves 2

2 tablespoons butter, melted

2 cloves garlic, peeled and minced

¼ teaspoon salt

20 medium radishes, ends trimmed, quartered

2 tablespoons goat cheese crumbles

1 tablespoon chopped fresh parsley

1   Preheat air fryer at 375°F for 3 minutes.

2   In a medium bowl, combine butter, garlic, and salt. Toss radishes in mixture.

3   Place radishes in ungreased air fryer basket. Cook 5 minutes. Shake basket, then cook an additional 5 minutes.

4   Transfer to a large serving dish. Toss with goat cheese and garnish with parsley. Serve warm.

PER SERVING

CALORIES: 153	FAT: 14g
PROTEIN: 3g	SODIUM: 367mg
FIBER: 2g	CARBOHYDRATES: 4g
NET CARBOHYDRATES: 3g	SUGAR: 2g

Prosciutto-Wrapped Asparagus

The air fryer knows how to crisp up prosciutto and there's no need for seasoning. The salty nature of prosciutto lends just enough flavor for these tasty spears.

- **Hands-On Time:** 10 minutes
- **Cook Time:** 12 minutes

Serves 4

3 ounces prosciutto, sliced lengthwise into 18 slices

18 thick asparagus spears, trimmed of woody ends

1 Spiral wrap the prosciutto strips from the bottom of the asparagus to the top, stopping before covering the tip.

2 Preheat air fryer at 400°F for 3 minutes.

3 Place wrapped asparagus in ungreased air fryer basket. Cook 6 minutes. Shake. Cook an additional 6 minutes until prosciutto is crisp.

4 Transfer to a plate and serve.

PER SERVING

CALORIES: 56	FAT: 2g
PROTEIN: 7g	SODIUM: 574mg
FIBER: 1g	CARBOHYDRATES: 3g
NET CARBOHYDRATES: 1g	SUGAR: 1g

Baked Fennel

Fennel's distinct anise, or licorice, flavor tends to tame once heated. Add a squeeze of lemon and this side dish is perfect alongside proteins like chicken.

- **Hands-On Time:** 5 minutes
- **Cook Time:** 8 minutes

Serves 2

1 large fennel bulb, fronds removed and reserved, sliced

2 teaspoons olive oil

¼ teaspoon salt

2 lemon wedges

1 tablespoon chopped fennel fronds

1 Preheat air fryer at 350°F for 3 minutes.

2 Brush fennel slices on both sides with olive oil and season with salt.

3 Place fennel slices in ungreased air fryer basket. Cook 8 minutes.

4 Transfer to a medium serving dish. Squeeze lemon on fennel and garnish with chopped fronds. Serve warm.

PER SERVING

CALORIES: 78	FAT: 5g
PROTEIN: 2g	SODIUM: 353mg
FIBER: 4g	CARBOHYDRATES: 9g
NET CARBOHYDRATES: 5g	SUGAR: 5g

Roasted Red Peppers

These peppers can be bought at stores, but why spend that money when they are so easy to make with your air fryer for pennies on the dollar? They can be added in salads, placed on pizzas, chopped up in deviled eggs, folded into frittatas, and used wherever else your imagination takes you.

- **Hands-On Time:** 10 minutes
- **Cook Time:** 24 minutes

Serves 2

2 large red bell peppers, tops and bottoms removed, cut along rib sections and seeded
2 tablespoons olive oil

THE MANY COLORS OF BELL PEPPERS

In addition to red bell peppers, there are also green, yellow, orange, and even white and purple. Follow the Roasted Red Peppers recipe using your pepper color of choice. Even switch it up from recipe to recipe. Each color yields different nutrient components, so check labels or look up nutritional information online. Variety is the spice of life: Give the variety of colors a chance and enhance your health benefits!

1 Preheat air fryer at 400°F for 3 minutes.

2 In a small bowl, toss pepper sections with olive oil.

3 Arrange sections in ungreased air fryer basket. Cook 12 minutes. Flip peppers and cook an additional 12 minutes.

4 Transfer peppers to a small metal bowl. Cover bowl with plastic wrap and let rest 15 minutes to allow further steaming to occur.

5 Remove peppers from bowl. Peel and discard skins from peppers. Serve.

PER SERVING

CALORIES: 170	FAT: 14g
PROTEIN: 2g	SODIUM: 7mg
FIBER: 3g	CARBOHYDRATES: 10g
NET CARBOHYDRATES: 7g	SUGAR: 7g

Spaghetti Squash with Avocado Carbonara

Spaghetti alla carbonara is a fantastically rich southern Italian meal. It almost tastes like an alfredo; however, there is no cream used. The creaminess comes from the eggs and the Parmesan cheese. In this dish, there is avocado added for healthy fat, and the carb-filled pasta is replaced with spaghetti squash.

- **Hands-On Time: 5 minutes**
- **Cook Time: 32 minutes**

Serves 4

2 teaspoons olive oil

1 (1½-pound) spaghetti squash, halved and seeded

1 medium ripe avocado, peeled and pitted

¼ cup chicken broth

1 large egg

2 tablespoons grated Parmesan cheese

¼ teaspoon salt

2 slices sugar-free bacon

¼ cup chopped fresh parsley

1 Preheat air fryer at 375°F for 3 minutes.

2 Rub olive oil over both halves of spaghetti squash. Place flat sides down in ungreased air fryer basket. Cook 25 minutes.

3 While squash is cooking, blend together avocado, chicken broth, egg, Parmesan cheese, and salt in a medium bowl. Set aside.

4 In a large skillet, cook bacon over medium heat 5 minutes until crispy. Transfer cooked bacon to a paper towel to cool 5 minutes, then crumble.

5 Transfer cooked squash to a cutting board and let cool 5 minutes until easy to handle. Using a fork, gently pull strands out of squash. Transfer strands to same skillet.

6 Add avocado mixture and parsley to skillet. Over medium heat, toss spaghetti squash with sauce 2 minutes until well coated. Add bacon crumbles.

7 Transfer to a large serving dish and serve warm.

PER SERVING

CALORIES: 185	FAT: 13g
PROTEIN: 6g	SODIUM: 364mg
FIBER: 6g	CARBOHYDRATES: 14g
NET CARBOHYDRATES: 9g	SUGAR: 4g

Parmesan Thyme Cauliflower

This recipe yields a nice cauliflower side dish that can be served with any protein of your choice. If you prefer your cauliflower a little more tender, just add a few minutes to your cooking time.

- **Hands-On Time: 10 minutes**
- **Cook Time: 12 minutes**

Serves 4

3 tablespoons butter, melted

2 tablespoons grated Parmesan cheese

2 teaspoons dried thyme

½ teaspoon garlic powder

¼ teaspoon salt

1 large head cauliflower, chopped into small florets

1 Preheat air fryer at 350°F for 3 minutes.

2 In a large bowl, combine butter, Parmesan cheese, thyme, garlic powder, and salt. Toss in florets.

3 Place half of cauliflower mixture in ungreased air fryer basket. Cook 3 minutes. Shake basket, then cook an additional 3 minutes.

4 Transfer cooked cauliflower to a large serving bowl. Repeat cooking with remaining cauliflower. Serve warm.

PER SERVING

CALORIES: 142	FAT: 10g
PROTEIN: 5g	SODIUM: 252mg
FIBER: 4g	CARBOHYDRATES: 11g
NET CARBOHYDRATES: 7g	SUGAR: 4g

Creamy Cauli-Root Vegetable Mash

Although mashed potatoes are a staple of a lot of American meals, there are many vegetables and tubers that can replicate that creamy mouthfeel without the carbs. If you want to load this mash up, add some cooked bacon crumbles and grated Cheddar cheese and cook for another minute or two!

- **Hands-On Time:** 10 minutes
- **Cook Time:** 15 minutes

Serves 4

1 small head cauliflower, chopped into small florets

1 medium rutabaga, peeled and small-diced

4 tablespoons butter, divided

1 teaspoon salt, divided

3 cloves garlic, peeled

½ teaspoon freshly ground black pepper

2 ounces cream cheese, room temperature

½ cup unsweetened almond milk

1 Preheat air fryer at 350°F for 3 minutes.

2 In a large bowl, toss cauliflower florets and rutabaga with 2 tablespoons melted butter and ½ teaspoon salt.

3 Place mixture in ungreased air fryer basket. Cook 5 minutes. Toss mixture, then cook an additional 5 minutes. Add garlic. Cook another 5 minutes.

4 Using a stand blender or food processor, blend or pulse cooked ingredients with remaining butter, remaining salt, pepper, cream cheese, and almond milk.

5 Transfer to a large serving dish and serve warm.

PER SERVING

CALORIES: 215	**FAT:** 17g
PROTEIN: 5g	**SODIUM:** 701mg
FIBER: 4g	**CARBOHYDRATES:** 13g
NET CARBOHYDRATES: 9g	**SUGAR:** 6g

Seasoned Green Beans

You know the scenario: You've gone to the store or farmers' market and bought a bag of beautiful fresh green beans...but now what? They sit in the refrigerator for a long time and get a little rotten—maybe never making their way to your dinner plate at all. The air fryer is a quick way to cook those green beans, so you can enjoy them in most any meal.

- **Hands-On Time: 5 minutes**
- **Cook Time: 10 minutes**

Serves 4

2 cups fresh green beans, ends trimmed

1 tablespoon butter, melted

½ teaspoon salt

¼ teaspoon freshly ground black pepper

1 slice sugar-free bacon, diced

1 clove garlic, peeled and minced

1 lemon wedge

1 Preheat air fryer at 375°F for 3 minutes.

2 In a medium bowl, toss together green beans, butter, salt, and pepper.

3 Add green beans to ungreased air fryer basket and cook 5 minutes. Toss in bacon and cook an additional 4 minutes. Toss in minced garlic and cook an additional minute.

4 Transfer to a medium serving dish, squeeze lemon over beans, and toss. Serve warm.

PER SERVING

CALORIES: 51	FAT: 4g
PROTEIN: 2g	SODIUM: 331mg
FIBER: 1g	CARBOHYDRATES: 4g
NET CARBOHYDRATES: 3g	SUGAR: 2g

Fried Artichoke Hearts

Because the artichoke hearts have already been softened and seasoned with salt and citrus from the lemon, it doesn't take much to flavor these fried vegetables. Serve as a side or atop a salad for a delicious change of pace.

- **Hands-On Time:** 10 minutes
- **Cook Time:** 14 minutes

Serves 4

1 large egg
1 tablespoon Dijon mustard
½ cup crushed pork rinds
¼ cup almond flour
1 (14.75-ounce) jar artichoke
    hearts in water, drained

1   Preheat air fryer at 350°F for 3 minutes.

2   In a medium bowl, whisk together egg and Dijon mustard.

3   In a separate shallow dish combine pork rinds and almond flour.

4   Dip artichoke hearts in egg mixture, then dredge in pork rind mixture.

5   Place half of prepared artichoke hearts in ungreased air fryer basket. Cook 7 minutes.

6   Transfer to a large serving plate and repeat cooking with remaining artichokes. Serve warm.

PER SERVING

CALORIES: 107	FAT: 6g
PROTEIN: 7g	SODIUM: 342mg
FIBER: 1g	CARBOHYDRATES: 6g
NET CARBOHYDRATES: 2g	SUGAR: 0g

Bacony Mushrooms and Onions

Make this quick side dish to serve over a steak or next to a grilled chicken breast.

- **Hands-On Time:** 10 minutes
- **Cook Time:** 9 minutes

Serves 4

16 ounces white button mushrooms, stems trimmed, halved

1 small yellow onion, peeled and sliced into half-moons

4 slices sugar-free bacon, diced

1 clove garlic, peeled and minced

1 Preheat air fryer at 350°F for 3 minutes.

2 Place mushrooms, onion, and bacon in ungreased air fryer basket. Cook 5 minutes. Toss, then cook another 3 minutes.

3 Add garlic to basket and cook an additional minute.

4 Transfer to a medium serving dish and serve warm.

PER SERVING

CALORIES: 63	FAT: 3g
PROTEIN: 6g	SODIUM: 151mg
FIBER: 1g	CARBOHYDRATES: 6g
NET CARBOHYDRATES: 4g	SUGAR: 3g

Seasoned Roasted Asparagus

Because asparagus comes in many thicknesses, watch your cook time when making this dish. As far as color, try the green, white, or even purple asparagus for this recipe.

- **Hands-On Time:** 5 minutes
- **Cook Time:** 9 minutes

Serves 6

1 pound (about 30) medium-thick asparagus spears, woody ends discarded

1 tablespoon butter, melted

¼ teaspoon salt

1 clove garlic, peeled and minced

2 teaspoons chopped fresh dill

1 Preheat air fryer at 375°F for 3 minutes.

2 In a large bowl, toss asparagus with butter.

3 Add asparagus to ungreased air fryer basket and cook 5 minutes. Toss, then cook an additional 4 minutes.

4 Transfer asparagus to a large serving dish and toss with salt, garlic, and dill until coated. Serve warm.

PER SERVING

CALORIES: 26	FAT: 2g
PROTEIN: 1g	SODIUM: 98mg
FIBER: 1g	CARBOHYDRATES: 2g
NET CARBOHYDRATES: 1g	SUGAR: 1g

Citrus Scallions

Often overlooked, this member of the *Allium* genus is more commonly used in Asian dishes. But, as most Southerners know, a little onion on the side of your plate is a treat. These small onions are quick and easy to cook, as well as much milder than a typical yellow onion.

- **Hands-On Time: 5 minutes**
- **Cook Time: 7 minutes**

Serves 6

2 bunches fresh scallions, ends trimmed to fit air fryer basket, halved lengthwise
1 tablespoon olive oil
2 teaspoons lime juice
¼ teaspoon salt
¼ teaspoon freshly ground black pepper
2 teaspoons lime zest

1 Preheat air fryer at 375°F for 3 minutes.

2 Toss scallions with olive oil and lime juice in a large bowl.

3 Add scallions to ungreased air fryer basket and cook 4 minutes. Toss, then cook an additional 3 minutes.

4 Transfer scallions to a large serving dish and toss with salt and pepper. Garnish with lime zest. Serve warm.

PER SERVING

CALORIES: 30	FAT: 2g
PROTEIN: 1g	SODIUM: 102mg
FIBER: 1g	CARBOHYDRATES: 2g
NET CARBOHYDRATES: 2g	SUGAR: 1g

WHAT ABOUT THE CHOPPED-OFF SCALLION GREENS?

Some of the top greens are going to be cut off for uniformity and to fit in your air fryer basket. But there is no need to throw these away: Place them in a container with water for up to one week, changing out the water every three days. These are a perfect flavor addition when making a bone broth or soup base.

Parsnips with Tahini Dressing

Parsnips are those carrot-looking white things that you may have passed by in the grocery store for years. They are of the same family as carrots, but unlike with edible carrot greens, do not eat parsnip greens.

- **Hands-On Time:** 10 minutes
- **Cook Time:** 10 minutes

Serves 4

For Parsnips
1 teaspoon olive oil
½ teaspoon salt
3 large parsnips, peeled, halved lengthwise, and cut into 1" half-moons

For Tahini Dressing
1 tablespoon tahini
1 tablespoon fresh lemon juice
1 teaspoon water
1 clove garlic, peeled and minced
1 tablespoon chopped fresh parsley

1 **To make Parsnips:** Preheat air fryer at 375°F for 3 minutes.

2 In a medium bowl, whisk together olive oil and salt. Add parsnips and toss.

3 Add parsnips to ungreased air fryer basket and cook 5 minutes. Toss, then cook an additional 5 minutes.

4 **To make Tahini Dressing:** While parsnips are cooking, whisk together tahini, lemon juice, water, and garlic in a medium bowl.

5 Add cooked parsnips and toss. Transfer to a medium serving dish. Garnish with parsley. Serve.

PER SERVING

CALORIES: 82	FAT: 3g
PROTEIN: 2g	SODIUM: 299mg
FIBER: 3g	CARBOHYDRATES: 13g
NET CARBOHYDRATES: 9g	SUGAR: 3g

Simple Roasted Garlic

It is amazing how, after roasting garlic bulbs, you can squeeze the garlic out of the peel like butter. Great mixed in with "fauxtato" mashes, dips, and even marinades, roasted garlic is magic—turning whatever it touches into gold!

- **Hands-On Time:** 10 minutes
- **Cook Time:** 45 minutes

Serves 8

¼ cup avocado oil

2 bulbs garlic, unpeeled, ¼" removed from top

⅛ teaspoon salt

1 Preheat air fryer at 350°F for 3 minutes.

2 Drizzle avocado oil over garlic bulbs and rub it in with your finger. Season each bulb with salt.

3 Roll each bulb up in a square of aluminum foil. Place wrapped bulbs in ungreased air fryer basket. Cook 45 minutes.

4 Unwrap each bulb. When cooled, squeeze roasted garlic from each clove and use as desired. Refrigerate unused bulbs in an airtight container up to three days.

PER SERVING

CALORIES: 31	**FAT:** 0g
PROTEIN: 1g	**SODIUM:** 2mg
FIBER: 0g	**CARBOHYDRATES:** 6g
NET CARBOHYDRATES: 6g	**SUGAR:** 0g

Chili Lime Avocado Halves

Perfect on a low-carb diet, avocado lends such a healthy dose of fat and nutrients to your meals. And in addition to being filling, the avocado becomes creamier when heated.

- **Hands-On Time: 5 minutes**
- **Cook Time: 7 minutes**

Serves 4

2 teaspoons olive oil
Juice of ½ medium lime
2 medium avocados, halved, pitted, and left in skins
1 teaspoon chili powder
¼ teaspoon salt

1 Preheat air fryer at 400°F for 3 minutes.

2 Combine olive oil and lime juice in a small bowl and brush over avocado halves.

3 Combine chili powder and salt in a separate small bowl. Sprinkle over avocado halves.

4 Place avocado halves, cut sides up, in ungreased air fryer basket. Cook 7 minutes.

5 Transfer to a serving plate and serve warm.

PER SERVING

CALORIES: 184		FAT: 17g	
PROTEIN: 2g		SODIUM: 172mg	
FIBER: 7g		CARBOHYDRATES: 9g	
NET CARBOHYDRATES: 2g		SUGAR: 1g	

Zucchini Ribbons

Just like pasta, Zucchini Ribbons can be a side dish or a main meal depending on how you treat them or what you put on top of them.

- **Hands-On Time: 10 minutes**
- **Cook Time: 3 minutes**

Serves 4

2 medium zucchini (seed core discarded), peeled into thin ribbons
2 teaspoons butter, melted
¼ teaspoon salt
¼ teaspoon freshly ground black pepper

1 Preheat air fryer at 275°F for 3 minutes.

2 In a medium bowl, toss zucchini ribbons with butter, salt, and pepper.

3 Place zucchini in ungreased air fryer basket and cook 1 minute. Toss and cook an additional 2 minutes.

4 Serve warm.

PER SERVING

CALORIES: 34		FAT: 2g	
PROTEIN: 1g		SODIUM: 153mg	
FIBER: 1g		CARBOHYDRATES: 3g	
NET CARBOHYDRATES: 2g		SUGAR: 2g	

Boursin-Stuffed Mushrooms

Boursin cheese has the consistency of cream cheese and is a product of Normandy. The magic of Boursin (and difference between cream cheese) is that it has already been seasoned for you. Boursin can be found with the specialty cheeses in the deli section of most grocers. It comes in a variety of flavors and can be used as a spread or in recipes such as this.

- **Hands-On Time:** 10 minutes
- **Cook Time:** 5 minutes

Serves 2

1 teaspoon olive oil

12 whole white button mushroom tops

2 tablespoons diced white button mushroom stems

1 tablespoon peeled and grated yellow onion

¼ cup herbed Boursin cheese

2 tablespoons crushed pork rinds

1 Brush olive oil around top ridge of each mushroom top.

2 Preheat air fryer at 350°F for 3 minutes.

3 In a small bowl, combine mushroom stems, onion, and Boursin cheese. Distribute and press mixture into tops of mushrooms. Sprinkle pork rinds on top.

4 Place stuffed mushrooms in ungreased air fryer basket. Cook 5 minutes. Serve warm.

PER SERVING

CALORIES: 178	FAT: 15g
PROTEIN: 7g	SODIUM: 202mg
FIBER: 1g	CARBOHYDRATES: 5g
NET CARBOHYDRATES: 4g	SUGAR: 3g

Baked Avocado with Burrata and Blistered Tomatoes

This dish is creamy times two: Avocado and Burrata cheese are two velvety powerhouses which, when served with fresh tomatoes and basil, will blow your mind.

- **Hands-On Time: 5 minutes**
- **Cook Time: 7 minutes**

Serves 4

8 medium cherry tomatoes
2 teaspoons olive oil
2 medium avocados, halved, pitted, and left in skins
¼ teaspoon salt
4 ounces Burrata cheese
2 tablespoons julienned fresh basil

WHAT IS BURRATA?

Burrata is like the molten lava cake of cheeses. Encased in beautiful fresh mozzarella, the interior has a creamy, buttery consistency. Made from buffalo or cow's milk, Burrata is becoming increasingly mainstream in America and can be found with the specialty cheeses in the deli section of most grocery stores. It is generally sold in a plastic container of milky liquid.

1. Preheat air fryer at 375°F for 3 minutes.

2. Toss tomatoes in olive oil in a small bowl.

3. Place avocado halves, cut sides up, in ungreased air fryer basket. Scatter tomatoes around avocado halves. Cook 7 minutes.

4. Place avocado halves on four small plates. Add two tomatoes to each half. Sprinkle salt over tomatoes. Tear Burrata cheese and evenly distribute over tomatoes. Garnish with basil. Serve.

PER SERVING

CALORIES: 269	FAT: 24g
PROTEIN: 7g	SODIUM: 240mg
FIBER: 7g	CARBOHYDRATES: 10g
NET CARBOHYDRATES: 3g	SUGAR: 2g

Broccoli Tots

Tots don't just have to be of the potato variety! Give these a try and just try to tell me your family hasn't fallen in love.

- **Hands-On Time:** 10 minutes
- **Cook Time:** 18 minutes

Serves 4

1 cup riced broccoli

1 large egg

⅓ cup grated sharp Cheddar cheese

1 ounce cream cheese, room temperature

1 tablespoon peeled and grated yellow onion

⅓ cup crushed pork rinds

½ teaspoon salt

¼ teaspoon garlic powder

WHERE DO I FIND BROCCOLI RICE?

Although premade broccoli rice can be purchased in most produce or frozen food sections, broccoli rice is actually very easy to make. The easiest way is to simply grate a head of broccoli on a box grater, or pulse in a food processor to desired consistency.

1 Preheat air fryer at 375°F for 3 minutes.

2 In a medium bowl, combine all ingredients. Form into twelve rectangular mounds (about 1 tablespoon each).

3 Cut a piece of parchment paper to fit bottom of air fryer basket. Place six pieces on parchment paper. Cook 9 minutes. Transfer to a medium serving plate and repeat cooking with remaining pieces.

4 Let rest 5 minutes, then serve warm.

PER SERVING

CALORIES: 102	FAT: 8g
PROTEIN: 7g	SODIUM: 449mg
FIBER: 1g	CARBOHYDRATES: 2g
NET CARBOHYDRATES: 1g	SUGAR: 1g

Crispy Zucchini Fries

These breaded Crispy Zucchini Fries are excellent on their own, but they're even better dipped in a creamy rémoulade. A healthy alternative to drive-through French fries, this treat is delicious!

- **Hands-On Time:** 10 minutes
- **Cook Time:** 20 minutes

Serves 2

1 large zucchini, cut into ¼" fries
1 teaspoon salt
1 large egg
1 tablespoon sour cream
½ cup almond flour
½ cup grated Parmesan cheese

TRY THIS RÉMOULADE FOR DIPPING!

To whip up your own delicious rémoulade, simply combine the following ingredients and refrigerate covered up to three days until ready to use: ½ cup mayonnaise, 1 tablespoon Dijon mustard, 1 teaspoon smoked paprika, 1 teaspoon Cajun seasoning, 1 teaspoon prepared horseradish, ½ teaspoon dill pickle juice, ½ teaspoon Tabasco original hot sauce, and 2 cloves peeled and minced garlic.

1 Scatter zucchini fries evenly over a paper towel. Sprinkle with salt. Let set 10 minutes to pull out moisture, then pat with paper towels.

2 Preheat air fryer to 375°F for 3 minutes.

3 Whisk egg and sour cream together in a small bowl.

4 Combine almond flour and Parmesan cheese in a separate shallow dish.

5 Dip zucchini in egg mixture. Dredge in flour mixture. Place half of zucchini in air fryer basket lightly greased with olive oil and cook 5 minutes. Flip fries, then cook an additional 5 minutes.

6 Transfer fries to a medium serving dish. Repeat with remaining zucchini fries and serve warm.

PER SERVING

CALORIES: 318	**FAT:** 24g
PROTEIN: 19g	**SODIUM:** 399mg
FIBER: 4g	**CARBOHYDRATES:** 12g
NET CARBOHYDRATES: 5g	**SUGAR:** 5g

Turnip Fries with Everything Bagel Seasoning

Have you ever wondered what to do with that weird little purplish-white orb in the produce section? Throw that turnip in your basket and give it a try with this tasty recipe. This root vegetable is loaded with fiber and nutrients and low in carbs!

- **Hands-On Time: 5 minutes**
- **Cook Time: 15 minutes**

Serves 4

2 medium turnips, peeled and cut into ¼" fries
2 teaspoons avocado oil
2 teaspoons Everything Bagel seasoning, divided

1 Preheat air fryer to 400°F for 3 minutes.

2 In a medium bowl, toss fries with avocado oil and 1 teaspoon seasoning.

3 Place fries in air fryer basket lightly greased with olive oil and cook 5 minutes. Shake basket and cook an additional 5 minutes. Shake, then cook another 5 minutes.

4 Transfer to a medium serving plate, garnish with remaining seasoning, and serve warm.

PER SERVING

CALORIES: 42	**FAT:** 3g
PROTEIN: 1g	**SODIUM:** 235mg
FIBER: 1g	**CARBOHYDRATES:** 4g
NET CARBOHYDRATES: 3g	**SUGAR:** 2g

Sesame Shishito Peppers

Although these mild peppers can be eaten raw, when you air fry them to get a little char, they are even better. Coupled with just a touch of sesame oil, these make a great side dish or snack.

- **Hands-On Time: 5 minutes**
- **Cook Time: 8 minutes**

Serves 2

6 ounces (about 3½ cups)
   shishito peppers
1 teaspoon sesame oil
1 teaspoon salt, divided
1 teaspoon sesame seeds

1 In a medium bowl, toss peppers with sesame oil and ½ teaspoon salt.

2 Preheat air fryer at 375°F for 3 minutes.

3 Add peppers to fryer basket and cook 4 minutes. Shake peppers. Cook an additional 4 minutes until peppers are blistered.

4 Transfer peppers to a serving dish and garnish with remaining salt and sesame seeds.

PER SERVING

CALORIES: 52	FAT: 3g
PROTEIN: 2g	SODIUM: 1,173mg
FIBER: 1g	CARBOHYDRATES: 4g
NET CARBOHYDRATES: 3g	SUGAR: 3g

WHAT ARE SHISHITO PEPPERS?
Move over edamame, these shishito peppers are the next best thing in super easy appetizers and are amazing to enjoy with friends over drinks. They're showing up more and more in common grocery stores, and the natural flavor of these mild and sweet chili peppers is enhanced and taken to the next level with a little oil, salt, and char.

Chicken Main Dishes

Living a low-carb life can be lonely sometimes when your options feel limited. While chicken is affordable and packed with protein, you might assume you are confined to bland, limp breasts and drumsticks to avoid the carbs. But that's simply not the case! If you miss fried chicken out of a bucket with a biscuit side, the air fryer is your new best friend. You are using a significantly lower amount of oil in the preparation, but the heat still gives it that crispiness on all sides. And because of the quicker cooking time, more nutrients stay intact and the chicken will be juicy and delicious.

Whether you're craving Cheesy Chicken Patties or your family is calling for Yogurt Curry Chicken Legs, this chapter has a chicken recipe for every occasion. From Spicy Yellow Mustard Wings to Barbecue Chicken Meatballs, your new favorites are calling—so get frying!

Prep Day Chicken Breasts

This recipe is prepared simply so that you can add the chicken breasts to a variety of other recipes. Cook them at the beginning of the week so they will be ready to add to a frittata, stir-fry, salad, or soup during the week—or just heat them up and enjoy a simple meal.

- **Hands-On Time: 5 minutes**
- **Cook Time: 9 minutes**

Serves 4

2 teaspoons olive oil

2 (½-pound) boneless, skinless chicken breasts

½ teaspoon salt

¼ teaspoon freshly ground black pepper

1 Preheat air fryer at 350°F for 3 minutes.

2 Brush olive oil lightly over tops and bottom of chicken. Season with salt and pepper.

3 Add chicken to ungreased air fryer basket and cook 4 minutes. Shake basket gently and flip chicken. Cook an additional 5 minutes. Using a meat thermometer, ensure internal temperature is at least 165°F.

4 Transfer chicken to a large serving plate and let rest 5 minutes, then chop into 1″ cubes and store covered and refrigerated up to one week.

PER SERVING

CALORIES: 156	FAT: 5g
PROTEIN: 26g	SODIUM: 342mg
FIBER: 0g	CARBOHYDRATES: 0g
NET CARBOHYDRATES: 0g	SUGAR: 0g

Pecan-Crusted Honey Mustard Chicken Breasts

Pulse your pecans into a meal instead of a flour; the chunkier texture will give a thicker coat. If you prefer a thinner coat, just pulse your pecans down a bit more. If you want to skip this step altogether, just purchase almond meal and proceed!

- **Hands-On Time: 5 minutes**
- **Cook Time: 25 minutes**

Serves 4

2 (6-ounce) boneless, skinless chicken breasts, halved lengthwise

¼ cup Low-Carb Honey Mustard (see recipe in Chapter 3)

¼ cup finely chopped pecans

1 Preheat air fryer at 350°F for 3 minutes.

2 Coat chicken with Low-Carb Honey Mustard.

3 Place pecans in a shallow dish. Dredge chicken in pecans.

4 Add chicken to air fryer basket lightly greased with olive oil and cook 10 minutes. Gently flip chicken and cook an additional 15 minutes. Using a meat thermometer, ensure internal temperature is at least 165°F.

5 Transfer chicken to a large serving plate and let rest 5 minutes before serving.

PER SERVING

CALORIES: 203	FAT: 13g
PROTEIN: 20g	SODIUM: 147mg
FIBER: 1g	CARBOHYDRATES: 3g
NET CARBOHYDRATES: 0g	SUGAR: 0g

Chicken Bulgogi with Riced Cauliflower and Pickled Cucumbers

Traditionally, bulgogi is a Korean barbecue beef dish; however, the dark meat of the chicken thigh is also a great venue for this delicious sauce. Coupled with the tameness of the cauliflower and the tanginess from the quick-pickled cucumbers, this is a complete one-bowl meal!

- **Hands-On Time:** 15 minutes
- **Cook Time:** 11 minutes

Serves 4

For Pickled Cucumbers
1 large English cucumber, thinly sliced
¼ cup apple cider vinegar
2 cloves garlic, peeled and minced
½ teaspoon ground ginger
⅛ teaspoon red pepper flakes
2 teaspoons granular erythritol
⅛ teaspoon salt

For Chicken Bulgogi
2 tablespoons coconut aminos
2 teaspoons sesame oil
2 teaspoons granular erythritol
1 tablespoon apple cider vinegar
1 tablespoon fresh lime juice
2 cloves garlic, peeled and minced
2 teaspoons peeled and minced fresh ginger
3 scallions, sliced, whites and greens separated, divided
1½ pounds (approximately 6) boneless, skinless chicken thighs, cut into 1" cubes

Additional Ingredients
4 cups steamed cauliflower rice
2 teaspoons roasted sesame seeds

1. **To make Pickled Cucumbers:** Combine all ingredients in a medium bowl. Cover and refrigerate until ready to serve.

2. **To make Chicken Bulgogi:** In a large bowl, whisk together coconut aminos, sesame oil, erythritol, apple cider vinegar, lime juice, garlic, ginger, and whites of scallions. Add chicken and marinate 10 minutes in refrigerator.

3. Preheat air fryer at 350°F for 3 minutes.

4. Using a slotted spoon, place chicken in ungreased air fryer basket. Do not discard excess marinade. Cook chicken 6 minutes. Shake basket and pour remaining marinade over chicken. Cook an additional 5 minutes. Using a meat thermometer, ensure internal temperature is at least 165°F.

5. **To assemble:** Serve chicken warm over steamed cauliflower in a large serving dish. Garnish with scallion greens, pickled cucumbers, and sesame seeds.

PER SERVING

CALORIES: 304	FAT: 8g
PROTEIN: 41g	SODIUM: 628mg
FIBER: 5g	CARBOHYDRATES: 15g
NET CARBOHYDRATES: 8g	SUGAR: 4g

Chicken Salad with Strawberries and Pecans

Whether you serve this on bread, in lettuce wraps, or straight off the spoon, the strawberries add such a fresh twist on this classic salad. The crunch from the pecans gives a textural element that adds another welcome surprise!

- **Hands-On Time:** 10 minutes
- **Cook Time:** 18 minutes

Serves 4

2 (approximately ½-pound) boneless, skinless chicken breasts, cut into 1" cubes

1 teaspoon salt

¼ teaspoon freshly ground black pepper

¾ cup mayonnaise

1 tablespoon fresh lime juice

½ cup chopped pecans

½ cup finely chopped celery

½ cup hulled and diced strawberries

1 Preheat air fryer at 350°F for 3 minutes.

2 Season chicken with salt and pepper.

3 Add chicken cubes in two batches to air fryer basket. Cook 4 minutes. Shake gently and flip chicken. Cook an additional 5 minutes. Check the chicken using a meat thermometer to ensure the internal temperature is at least 165°F.

4 Transfer to a plate and cool.

5 Chop chicken and add to a medium bowl. Add remaining ingredients and combine well. Refrigerate covered until ready to eat.

PER SERVING

CALORIES: 522	FAT: 44g
PROTEIN: 27g	SODIUM: 906mg
FIBER: 2g	CARBOHYDRATES: 5g
NET CARBOHYDRATES: 3g	SUGAR: 2g

Seasoned Chicken Legs

Keep the skin on the chicken legs; not only is it delicious, but it will hold the seasoning better and crisp up in the air fryer. Sooo tasty!

- **Hands-On Time:** 10 minutes
- **Cook Time:** 36 minutes

Serves 4

1 teaspoon baking powder
1 teaspoon dried mustard
1 teaspoon smoked paprika
1 teaspoon garlic powder
1 teaspoon salt
1 teaspoon freshly ground
  black pepper
1½ pounds (approximately 6)
  chicken legs
3 tablespoons butter, melted

1 Preheat air fryer at 375°F for 3 minutes.

2 In a large bowl, combine baking powder, dried mustard, paprika, garlic powder, salt, and pepper. Add chicken and toss until coated.

3 Add half of chicken to air fryer basket lightly greased with olive oil and cook 10 minutes.

4 Brush chicken lightly with melted butter, then flip and brush other side. Cook an additional 8 minutes. Using a meat thermometer, ensure internal temperature is at least 165°F.

5 Transfer chicken to a large serving plate and let rest 5 minutes. Repeat cooking with remaining chicken and serve warm.

PER SERVING

CALORIES: 246	**FAT:** 17g
PROTEIN: 21g	**SODIUM:** 760mg
FIBER: 0g	**CARBOHYDRATES:** 2g
NET CARBOHYDRATES: 1g	**SUGAR:** 0g

Yogurt Curry Chicken Legs

This Indian-inspired dish may be limited in ingredients, but it's overflowing with flavors. The fragrant, richly spiced tomato sauce coats the mild taste of chicken. It is an easy dish to make at home.

- **Hands-On Time:** 10 minutes
- **Cook Time:** 36 minutes

Serves 4

¾ cup plain Greek yogurt

1 tablespoon no-sugar-added tomato paste

2 teaspoons curry powder

1 teaspoon salt

1½ pounds (approximately 6) chicken legs

2 tablespoons chopped fresh mint

1 In a medium bowl, whisk together yogurt, tomato paste, curry powder, and salt. Divide mixture in half. Cover half and place in refrigerator. Add chicken to other half and toss until coated. Cover and refrigerate 30 minutes up to overnight.

2 Preheat air fryer at 375°F for 3 minutes.

3 Shake excess marinade from chicken. Add half of chicken to air fryer basket lightly greased with olive oil and cook 10 minutes.

4 Brush chicken lightly with extra yogurt mixture. Flip and brush other side. Cook an additional 8 minutes. Using a meat thermometer, ensure internal temperature is at least 165°F.

5 Transfer chicken to a large serving plate and let rest 5 minutes. Repeat cooking with remaining chicken and serve warm garnished with mint.

PER SERVING

CALORIES: 298	**FAT:** 15g
PROTEIN: 34g	**SODIUM:** 455mg
FIBER: 0g	**CARBOHYDRATES:** 6g
NET CARBOHYDRATES: 6g	**SUGAR:** 6g

Garlic Parm Wings

If you use your air fryer for only one food, make it chicken wings! The convection heat cooks up that chicken skin from all sides, making each bite equally crispy on the outside and juicy on the inside.

- **Hands-On Time:** 10 minutes
- **Cook Time:** 22 minutes

Serves 4

1 tablespoon water

2 pounds chicken wings, split at the joint

2 tablespoons melted butter, divided

2 tablespoons grated Parmesan cheese

4 cloves garlic, peeled and minced

¼ teaspoon salt

HOW TO SEPARATE CHICKEN WINGS

Some grocery stores will have the wings already broken down for the consumer; however, more often you will have to purchase whole wings. To separate the wing into the different parts, first stretch it out. There will be two cuts to each wing, yielding three parts: the drumette, the wingette, and the tip. Using kitchen shears or a sharp knife, cut the wing at each joint.

1 Pour water into bottom of air fryer to ensure minimum smoke from fat drippings. Preheat air fryer at 250°F for 3 minutes.

2 In a large bowl, toss wings in 1 tablespoon butter. Place wings in ungreased air fryer basket and cook 6 minutes. Flip and cook an additional 6 minutes.

3 While wings are cooking, combine remaining butter, Parmesan cheese, garlic, and salt in a separate large bowl.

4 Raise temperature on air fryer to 400°F. Flip wings and cook another 5 minutes. Flip once more and cook 5 more minutes.

5 Transfer to bowl with sauce and toss, then transfer to a large serving plate and serve warm.

PER SERVING

CALORIES: 300	**FAT:** 22g
PROTEIN: 23g	**SODIUM:** 292mg
FIBER: 0g	**CARBOHYDRATES:** 1g
NET CARBOHYDRATES: 1g	**SUGAR:** 0g

Cajun Breaded Drumettes

The drumette is the portion of the chicken wing that looks like a smaller chicken leg. The tanginess of the sour cream added to the heavy cream mimics the traditional buttermilk used in carb-filled breaded drumettes. Paired with the Cajun seasoning, this Southern dish is over-the-top!

- **Hands-On Time: 10 minutes**
- **Cook Time: 40 minutes**

Serves 4

1 pound chicken drumettes
½ cup cassava flour
½ cup heavy cream
½ cup sour cream
½ cup crushed pork rinds
1 tablespoon Cajun seasoning
2 tablespoons melted butter

1 In a large bowl, toss drumettes in cassava flour. Shake away excess flour and set aside.

2 In a medium bowl, whisk together heavy cream and sour cream. In a separate shallow dish, combine pork rinds and Cajun seasoning.

3 Preheat air fryer at 375°F for 3 minutes.

4 Dip floured drumettes in cream mixture. Dredge in seasoned pork rinds. Place half of drumettes in air fryer basket lightly greased with olive oil and cook 12 minutes.

5 Gently flip chicken and brush with 1 tablespoon butter. Cook an additional 8 minutes. Using a meat thermometer, ensure internal temperature is at least 165°F.

6 Transfer chicken to a large serving plate and let rest 5 minutes. Repeat cooking with remaining chicken and serve warm.

PER SERVING

CALORIES: 481	FAT: 38g
PROTEIN: 23g	SODIUM: 174mg
FIBER: 1g	CARBOHYDRATES: 13g
NET CARBOHYDRATES: 12g	SUGAR: 2g

Bangin' Chicken Wings

You may have heard of or even tried the popular Bang Bang Shrimp served in many restaurants. This is a healthier take that you'll love just as much!

- **Hands-On Time:** 10 minutes
- **Cook Time:** 22 minutes

Serves 4

2 tablespoons sesame oil
¼ teaspoon fish sauce
2 teaspoons coconut aminos
2 teaspoons sambal oelek
1 teaspoon granular erythritol
1 teaspoon fresh lime juice
2 pounds chicken wings, split at the joint
1 tablespoon water

WHAT IS SAMBAL OELEK?

Sambal oelek is an Indonesian chili paste usually containing salt, vinegar, and a variety of other spices. Found at most grocers in the ethnic foods aisle, it actually has the same ingredients and heat level as sriracha, but with zero sugars, so it's perfect for a low-carb diet!

1   Combine sesame oil, fish sauce, coconut aminos, sambal oelek, erythritol, and lime juice in a medium bowl. Divide mixture in half. Toss wings in half of sauce, cover, and refrigerate 30 minutes. Cover and refrigerate other half.

2   Preheat air fryer at 250°F for 3 minutes. Place water in bottom of air fryer to ensure minimum smoke from fat drippings. Place wings in ungreased air fryer basket and cook 6 minutes. Flip wings and cook an additional 6 minutes.

3   Raise temperature on air fryer to 400°F. Flip wings and cook 5 minutes. Flip wings once more and cook an additional 5 minutes.

4   Transfer wings to bowl with remaining sauce and toss. Serve.

PER SERVING

CALORIES: 298		**FAT:** 23g	
PROTEIN: 22g		**SODIUM:** 178mg	
FIBER: 0g		**CARBOHYDRATES:** 2g	
NET CARBOHYDRATES: 1g		**SUGAR:** 1g	

Spicy Yellow Mustard Wings

With a bit of Asian flair, these spicy wings are screaming to be eaten with friends alongside a few cold brews. Double or triple this recipe depending on the size of your group!

- **Hands-On Time:** 10 minutes
- **Cook Time:** 22 minutes

Serves 4

1 tablespoon water

2 pounds chicken wings, split at the joint

1 tablespoon sesame oil

2 tablespoons spicy yellow mustard

1 tablespoon coconut aminos

1 teaspoon granular erythritol

1 teaspoon apple cider vinegar

SPICY YELLOW MUSTARD HACK!

Because this recipe calls for a relatively nominal amount of mustard, you can save your dollars. Just go to your takeout drawer and grab some of those plastic packets already filled with that savory, spicy mustard that you probably already have left over from takeout orders.

1 Preheat air fryer at 250°F for 3 minutes. Pour water in bottom of air fryer to ensure minimum smoke from fat drippings.

2 In a large bowl, toss wings in sesame oil. Place in ungreased air fryer basket and cook 6 minutes. Flip wings and cook an additional 6 minutes.

3 While wings are cooking, combine mustard, coconut aminos, erythritol, and apple cider vinegar in a separate large bowl.

4 Raise temperature on air fryer to 400°F. Flip wings and cook 5 minutes. Flip again and cook an additional 5 minutes.

5 Transfer wings to bowl with sauce and toss. Serve.

PER SERVING

CALORIES: 272	**FAT:** 19g
PROTEIN: 22g	**SODIUM:** 253mg
FIBER: 0g	**CARBOHYDRATES:** 2g
NET CARBOHYDRATES: 1g	**SUGAR:** 1g

Cheesy Chicken Patties

The addition of onion and cheese in this recipe lends a moistness and creaminess to counter the low-fat meat, and it gives a flavor that blends well with the simply seasoned salt and pepper.

- **Hands-On Time:** 10 minutes
- **Cook Time:** 26 minutes

Serves 4

1 pound ground chicken

2 tablespoons peeled and diced yellow onion

¼ cup shredded Cheddar cheese

¼ cup chopped fresh parsley

1 large egg white, beaten

¼ teaspoon salt

¼ teaspoon freshly ground black pepper

VARIETIES OF GROUND CHICKEN

Ground chicken comes in varieties of white meat, dark meat, and a combination of both. Dark meat has more natural fat, which gives more flavor and moistness to the patty, though any chicken variety is acceptable for this recipe. And don't count out grinding up the chicken yourself if you are feeling adventurous!

1 Preheat air fryer at 350°F for 3 minutes.

2 In a large bowl, combine all ingredients and form into four patties, making a slight indentation in the middle of each patty. (Patties tend to puff up in the middle during the cooking process, so making an indentation will ensure the patty doesn't become a meatball.)

3 Add two patties to air fryer basket lightly greased with olive oil and cook 6 minutes. Flip patties and cook an additional 7 minutes, until internal temperature is at least 165°F. Transfer cooked patties to a large serving plate and repeat cooking with remaining patties.

4 Serve warm.

PER SERVING

CALORIES: 199	**FAT:** 12g
PROTEIN: 22g	**SODIUM:** 276mg
FIBER: 0g	**CARBOHYDRATES:** 1g
NET CARBOHYDRATES: 1g	**SUGAR:** 0g

Chicken and Goat Cheese Balls

Ground chicken can be a bit dry, but with the addition of the onion and goat cheese, these lean, mean Chicken and Goat Cheese Balls are just what the doctor ordered!

- **Hands-On Time:** 10 minutes
- **Cook Time:** 24 minutes

Serves 4

1 pound ground chicken
2 tablespoons peeled and grated yellow onion
¼ cup chopped fresh basil leaves
⅓ cup goat cheese crumbles
½ cup ground pork rinds
½ teaspoon garlic powder

1 Preheat air fryer at 350°F for 3 minutes.

2 In a large bowl, combine all ingredients and form into eighteen meatballs, about 2 tablespoons each.

3 Add half of balls to air fryer basket lightly greased with olive oil. Cook 6 minutes. Shake basket and cook an additional 6 minutes.

4 Transfer cooked balls to a serving plate and repeat cooking with remaining balls. Serve warm.

PER SERVING

CALORIES: 230	FAT: 14g
PROTEIN: 25g	SODIUM: 192mg
FIBER: 0g	CARBOHYDRATES: 1g
NET CARBOHYDRATES: 1g	SUGAR: 0g

Salsa Chicken

This is absolutely the easiest, tastiest, and lowest-calorie meal you can prepare in minutes on the hour. Trust your own heat-o-meter when choosing your salsa, or make some fruit salsas instead.

- **Hands-On Time:** 5 minutes
- **Cook Time:** 30 minutes

Serves 2

1 pound (approximately 4) boneless, skinless chicken thighs
1 cup mild chunky salsa

1 Preheat air fryer at 350°F for 3 minutes.

2 Place chicken thighs in square cake barrel. Cover with salsa.

3 Cook 30 minutes. Using a meat thermometer, ensure that the chicken is at least 165°F. Cook another minute if necessary.

4 Transfer to a serving plate and let rest 5 minutes. Serve warm.

PER SERVING

CALORIES: 309	FAT: 6g
PROTEIN: 53g	SODIUM: 1,012mg
FIBER: 2g	CARBOHYDRATES: 8g
NET CARBOHYDRATES: 6g	SUGAR: 5g

Barbecue Chicken Meatballs

These delectable meatballs are filled with barbecue flavor down to the pork rinds. If you can't get your hands on barbecue-flavored pork rinds, just substitute the plain variety; they will still work. Also, add a little cayenne pepper to the mix if you like the heat!

- **Hands-On Time:** 10 minutes
- **Cook Time:** 16 minutes

Serves 4

1 pound ground chicken

1 large egg

½ cup crushed barbecue-flavored pork rinds

1 tablespoon sour cream

2 teaspoons brown mustard

2 tablespoons peeled and grated yellow onion

2 tablespoons no-sugar-added tomato paste

1 teaspoon ground cumin

1 teaspoon chili powder

1 Preheat air fryer at 350°F for 3 minutes.

2 Combine all ingredients in a large bowl. Form into eighteen meatballs, about 2 tablespoons each.

3 Add half of meatballs to air fryer basket lightly greased with olive oil and cook 6 minutes. Shake basket and cook an additional 2 minutes.

4 Transfer cooked meatballs to a large serving dish and repeat cooking with remaining meatballs. Serve warm.

PER SERVING

CALORIES: 216	FAT: 13g	
PROTEIN: 24g	SODIUM: 208mg	
FIBER: 1g	CARBOHYDRATES: 2g	
NET CARBOHYDRATES: 1g	SUGAR: 1g	

Strawberry Basil–Glazed Chicken Tenders

Sweet and savory *and* salty—yes please! This is the chicken meal that your kids will scream for more of. Switch up your flavors by experimenting with different herbs and the variety of sugar-free jams and preserves available!

- **Hands-On Time:** 10 minutes
- **Cook Time:** 9 minutes

Serves 4

¼ cup sugar-free strawberry preserves

3 tablespoons chopped fresh basil, divided

1 teaspoon pulp-free orange juice

¼ teaspoon salt

¼ teaspoon freshly ground black pepper

1 pound chicken tenderloins

WHAT IS A CHICKEN TENDERLOIN?

You can generally find ready-to-eat chicken tenderloins already cut in the frozen chicken section. If not, just cut 1" slices from a chicken breast: It's the same thing. Also, you can often save a few bucks by cutting your own!

1 In a medium bowl, combine preserves, 2 tablespoons basil, orange juice, salt, and pepper. Add chicken. Cover and refrigerate 30 minutes up to overnight.

2 Preheat air fryer at 350°F for 3 minutes.

3 Add chicken to ungreased air fryer basket and cook 4 minutes. Shake gently and flip chicken. Cook an additional 5 minutes. Using a meat thermometer, ensure internal temperature is at least 165°F.

4 Transfer chicken to a large serving plate and let rest 5 minutes, then garnish with remaining basil and serve warm.

PER SERVING

CALORIES: 172	FAT: 3g
PROTEIN: 26g	SODIUM: 196mg
FIBER: 0g	CARBOHYDRATES: 13g
NET CARBOHYDRATES: 1g	SUGAR: 1g

Chicken Ratatouille Stir-Fry

Ratatouille is a French stewed dish with tomatoes, eggplant, zucchini, and peppers. This air fryer version with chicken gives you a full meal in just minutes, much less time than the traditional stew would take to make.

- **Hands-On Time: 15 minutes**
- **Cook Time: 15 minutes**

Serves 4

1 pound boneless, skinless chicken thighs, cut into 1" cubes

1 small eggplant, cut into 1" cubes

1 medium zucchini, cut into 1" cubes

1 small yellow bell pepper, seeded and diced

1 teaspoon salt

1 teaspoon Italian seasoning

2 tablespoons olive oil

1 (14.5-ounce) can diced tomatoes, including juice

2 tablespoons grated Parmesan cheese

2 tablespoons julienned fresh basil leaves

1   Preheat air fryer at 400°F for 3 minutes.

2   In a large bowl, combine chicken, eggplant, zucchini, bell pepper, salt, Italian seasoning, and olive oil.

3   Add chicken and vegetables to ungreased air fryer basket and cook 7 minutes.

4   Transfer chicken mixture to an ungreased cake barrel. Stir in tomatoes with juice. Cook an additional 8 minutes. Using a meat thermometer, ensure internal temperature is at least 165°F.

5   Transfer to a large serving dish. Toss with Parmesan cheese and garnish with basil. Serve.

PER SERVING

CALORIES: 247	FAT: 12g
PROTEIN: 25g	SODIUM: 843mg
FIBER: 3g	CARBOHYDRATES: 7g
NET CARBOHYDRATES: 5g	SUGAR: 5g

Sweet and Spicy Chicken Bites

Serve this sweet and spicy dish as is, over cauliflower rice, or in lettuce wraps. In addition, you can serve it up in takeout boxes purchased online or in most craft stores—just don't forget the chopsticks to round out the experience!

- **Hands-On Time:** 15 minutes
- **Cook Time:** 15 minutes

Serves 4

1 large egg

1 teaspoon water

4 tablespoons arrowroot flour

1 pound boneless, skinless chicken thighs, cut into 1" cubes

1 teaspoon sesame oil

2 teaspoons apple cider vinegar

2 tablespoons coconut aminos

3 cloves garlic, peeled and minced

2 teaspoons peeled and grated fresh ginger

2 teaspoons chili garlic sauce

2 teaspoons granular erythritol

¼ teaspoon salt

¼ teaspoon freshly ground white pepper

1 green onion, thinly sliced at a diagonal

1   Preheat air fryer at 400°F for 3 minutes.

2   In a medium bowl, whisk together egg, water, and arrowroot flour. Add chicken pieces and toss until fully coated.

3   In a large bowl, whisk together sesame oil, apple cider vinegar, coconut aminos, garlic, ginger, chili garlic sauce, erythritol, salt, and pepper. Set aside.

4   Add chicken to air fryer basket lightly greased with olive oil and cook 15 minutes, flipping chicken every 5 minutes.

5   Transfer cooked chicken to bowl with marinade and gently toss to coat.

6   Transfer to a large serving plate, garnish with green onion, and serve.

PER SERVING

CALORIES: 209	FAT: 7g
PROTEIN: 24g	SODIUM: 408mg
FIBER: 1g	CARBOHYDRATES: 12g
NET CARBOHYDRATES: 10g	SUGAR: 2g

Chicken Fajita Bowl

Move over, crunchy taco shells: We don't need you anymore. This complete fajita bowl is bursting with Mexican flavors—without the carb explosion usually associated with Taco Tuesday.

- **Hands-On Time: 15 minutes**
- **Cook Time: 16 minutes**

Serves 4

1 tablespoon olive oil
2 teaspoons arrowroot flour
¼ teaspoon chili powder
¼ teaspoon salt
¼ teaspoon smoked paprika
¼ teaspoon ground cumin
½ teaspoon granular erythritol
⅛ teaspoon onion powder
⅛ teaspoon garlic powder
1 pound boneless, skinless chicken breasts, cut into 3"-long strips
4 medium Roma tomatoes, cored, seeded, and diced
1 medium jalapeño, sliced and seeded
¼ cup peeled and diced red onion
½ cup queso fresco crumbles
4 tablespoons sour cream
1 medium avocado, peeled, pitted, and diced

1 In a large bowl, whisk together olive oil, arrowroot flour, chili powder, salt, paprika, cumin, erythritol, onion powder, and garlic powder. Add chicken strips and toss. Refrigerate covered 30 minutes up to overnight.

2 Preheat air fryer at 400°F for 3 minutes.

3 Add half of chicken to ungreased air fryer basket and cook 4 minutes. Shake basket. Cook an additional 4 minutes. Using a meat thermometer, ensure internal temperature is at least 165°F.

4 Transfer cooked chicken to two medium bowls and repeat cooking with remaining chicken.

5 Transfer remaining chicken to two more medium bowls. Add tomatoes, jalapeño, red onion, queso fresco cheese, sour cream, and avocado to bowls. Serve.

PER SERVING

CALORIES: 349	FAT: 20g
PROTEIN: 31g	SODIUM: 330mg
FIBER: 5g	CARBOHYDRATES: 13g
NET CARBOHYDRATES: 7g	SUGAR: 5g

PICKLED JALAPEÑO SLICES

Pickled jalapeño slices would be a great accent to this dish. Just slice and seed a large jalapeño and add to a small bowl with 2 tablespoons apple cider vinegar, 1 tablespoon warm water, and 1 teaspoon granular erythritol. Drain the liquid when ready to add to your dish.

Grilled Chicken Cobb Salad

Whether you are looking for lunch or dinner, this salad is stocked with delicious fillers, making it a complete meal. Also, if you have leftover chicken from the beginning of the week, use it up in this easy-to-put-together salad!

- **Hands-On Time:** 10 minutes
- **Cook Time:** 18 minutes

Serves 4

2 (approximately ½-pound) boneless, skinless chicken breasts, cut into 1" cubes

1 tablespoon avocado oil

½ teaspoon salt

¼ teaspoon freshly ground black pepper

4 cups chopped romaine lettuce

2 tablespoons olive oil

1 tablespoon fresh lemon juice

2 Air-Fried Hard-"Boiled" Eggs, sliced (see recipe in Chapter 2)

4 pieces sugar-free bacon, cooked and crumbled

2 medium Roma tomatoes, cored, seeded, and diced

¼ cup blue cheese crumbles

¼ cup peeled and diced red onion

1 large avocado, peeled, pitted, and diced

1 Preheat air fryer at 350°F for 3 minutes.

2 In a large bowl, toss chicken cubes with avocado oil. Season with salt and pepper.

3 Add half of chicken cubes to ungreased air fryer basket. Cook 4 minutes. Shake gently and flip chicken. Cook an additional 5 minutes. Using a meat thermometer, ensure internal temperature is at least 165°F.

4 Transfer cooked chicken to a large plate. Repeat cooking with remaining chicken.

5 In a separate large bowl, toss romaine lettuce with olive oil and lemon juice. Distribute into four medium bowls.

6 Garnish salads with remaining ingredients, including cooked chicken. Serve.

PER SERVING

CALORIES: 427	FAT: 28g
PROTEIN: 35g	SODIUM: 632mg
FIBER: 5g	CARBOHYDRATES: 9g
NET CARBOHYDRATES: 5g	SUGAR: 3g

Dilly Chicken Salad

This is the perfect meal to make and take along for a family outing—just stow beside a frozen ice pack and then enjoy this fresh meal out in nature!

- **Hands-On Time:** 10 minutes
- **Cook Time:** 18 minutes

Serves 4

2 (approximately ½-pound) boneless, skinless chicken breasts, cut into 1" cubes

½ teaspoon salt

¼ teaspoon freshly ground black pepper

¾ cup mayonnaise

1 tablespoon fresh lime juice

2 tablespoons chopped fresh dill

½ cup halved seedless red grapes

½ cup finely chopped celery

1 medium shallot, peeled and diced

1 Preheat air fryer at 350°F for 3 minutes.

2 Season chicken with salt and pepper. Add half of chicken cubes to ungreased air fryer basket. Cook 4 minutes. Shake gently and flip chicken. Cook an additional 5 minutes. Using a meat thermometer, ensure internal temperature is at least 165°F.

3 Transfer cooked chicken to a large plate. Repeat cooking with remaining chicken.

4 Toss chicken into a large serving bowl with remaining ingredients. Refrigerate covered 1 hour up to overnight until ready to eat.

PER SERVING

CALORIES: 440	FAT: 34g
PROTEIN: 26g	SODIUM: 616mg
FIBER: 1g	CARBOHYDRATES: 6g
NET CARBOHYDRATES: 5g	SUGAR: 4g

Tandoori-Inspired Chicken Kebabs

These beautifully spiced Indian chicken kebabs are excellent served over some steamed riced cauliflower or in lettuce wraps with some homemade sugar-free chutney. Have fun incorporating the chicken into your own creations.

- **Hands-On Time:** 15 minutes
- **Cook Time:** 24 minutes

Serves 4

1 small yellow onion, peeled and diced

1 (2") knob fresh ginger, peeled and minced

2 tablespoons fresh lime juice

1 cup canned unsweetened coconut milk

2 tablespoons no-sugar-added tomato paste

2 tablespoons olive oil

1 tablespoon ground cumin

1 tablespoon ground coriander

1 teaspoon cayenne pepper

1 teaspoon ground turmeric

2 teaspoons salt

1 pound boneless, skinless chicken thighs, cut into 1" cubes

2 tablespoons chopped fresh mint leaves

1 In a medium bowl, combine all ingredients except chicken and mint leaves. Add chicken pieces and toss until fully coated. Refrigerate covered 2 hours up to overnight.

2 Preheat air fryer at 350°F for 3 minutes.

3 Skewer chicken on eight skewers and place half of skewers on a kebab rack. Place rack in air fryer basket and cook 12 minutes. Discard marinade.

4 Transfer cooked kebabs to a large serving dish. Repeat cooking with remaining skewers. Garnish with mint leaves and serve.

PER SERVING

CALORIES: 150	FAT: 4g
PROTEIN: 26g	SODIUM: 402mg
FIBER: 0g	CARBOHYDRATES: 1g
NET CARBOHYDRATES: 1g	SUGAR: 0g

Honey Mustard Chicken Skewers

Chicken, vegetables, and honey mustard: Who needs a drive-through when this healthy, delicious meal can be ready in about 30 minutes with minimal prep.

- **Hands-On Time:** 10 minutes
- **Cook Time:** 24 minutes

Serves 4

1 pound boneless, skinless chicken thighs, cut into 1" cubes

½ cup Low-Carb Honey Mustard (see recipe in Chapter 3)

½ medium red onion, peeled and chopped into 1" pieces

1 medium green bell pepper, seeded and chopped into 1" pieces

2 tablespoons chopped fresh parsley

1 In a medium bowl, combine chicken cubes and Low-Carb Honey Mustard. Refrigerate covered 30 minutes.

2 Preheat air fryer at 350°F for 3 minutes.

3 Skewer chicken and vegetables alternately on eight skewers and place half of skewers on a kebab rack. Place rack in air fryer basket and cook 12 minutes.

4 Transfer cooked kebabs to a large serving dish. Repeat cooking with remaining skewers. Garnish with fresh parsley and serve warm.

PER SERVING

CALORIES: 259		FAT: 15g	
PROTEIN: 26g		SODIUM: 271mg	
FIBER: 1g		CARBOHYDRATES: 7g	
NET CARBOHYDRATES: 3g		SUGAR: 2g	

Dijon "Maple"-Glazed Cornish Hen

Just a touch of the maple extract, which can be found next to the vanilla extract in most grocery stores, is all you need to trick your taste buds into thinking you've added some thick maple syrup to your mustard.

- **Hands-On Time: 10 minutes**
- **Cook Time: 28 minutes**

Serves 2

2 tablespoons butter, melted

2 tablespoons Dijon mustard

½ teaspoon salt

½ teaspoon freshly ground black pepper

⅛ teaspoon ground nutmeg

½ teaspoon granular erythritol

⅛ teaspoon maple extract

1 tablespoon olive oil

1 (approximately 1¼-pound) Cornish game hen

1 small clementine, quartered

1 Preheat air fryer at 350°F for 3 minutes.

2 In a small bowl, combine butter, mustard, salt, pepper, nutmeg, erythritol, and maple extract.

3 Rub oil over and inside Cornish game hen. Sprinkle hen with seasoning mixture. Stuff clementine into hen's cavity.

4 Place hen in ungreased air fryer basket. Cook 10 minutes. Flip hen. Cook another 10 minutes. Flip hen and cook an additional 8 minutes. Using a meat thermometer, ensure internal temperature is at least 165°F.

5 Transfer hen to a cutting board and let rest 5 minutes. Once cool enough to handle, split in half by cutting down the spine. Serve warm.

PER SERVING

CALORIES: 543	**FAT:** 43g
PROTEIN: 30g	**SODIUM:** 1,029mg
FIBER: 1g	**CARBOHYDRATES:** 6g
NET CARBOHYDRATES: 4g	**SUGAR:** 3g

6

Beef and Pork Main Dishes

Naturally low-carb, beef and pork crisp up nicely in the air fryer and make fantastic additions to your low-carb diet. Packing tons of protein and naturally healthy fats, two of the three macronutrients your body needs to survive, these are two foods you won't want to skip over. And thanks to the air fryer, you have dozens of easy, delicious options for both!

With recipes ranging from Strip Steak with Mushrooms and Onions and Chopped Steakhouse Salad to Inside Out Barbecue Sliders and Buffalo-Style Pork Meatballs, this chapter will help get you started on some classic air fryer beef and pork recipes, and also introduce you to some new soon-to-be favorites. Enjoy!

Texas Rib Eye Steak

Also known as a *Cowboy Steak*, the rib eye is a rugged cut of meat that takes on the barbecue sauce in this recipe like a boss. Savory, spicy, *and* salty, this dish is perfect served with a refreshing coleslaw or creamy cauliflower mash.

- **Hands-On Time: 10 minutes**
- **Cook Time: 10 minutes**

Serves 2

1 tablespoon water

¼ cup sugar-free barbecue sauce

1 clove garlic, peeled and minced

⅛ teaspoon cayenne pepper

1 (12-ounce, 1"-thick) rib eye steak

1 Preheat air fryer at 400°F for 3 minutes. Pour water in bottom of air fryer to ensure minimum smoke from fat drippings.

2 Combine barbecue sauce, garlic, and cayenne pepper in a small bowl. Divide in half. Slather steak with half of sauce.

3 Place steak in air fryer basket lightly greased with olive oil. Cook 5 minutes. Flip steak. Brush with remaining sauce and cook an additional 5 minutes or until desired doneness.

4 Transfer steak to a cutting board and let rest 5 minutes, then slice and serve.

PER SERVING

CALORIES: 266	FAT: 12g
PROTEIN: 35g	SODIUM: 284mg
FIBER: 0g	CARBOHYDRATES: 3g
NET CARBOHYDRATES: 3g	SUGAR: 11g

Strip Steak with Mushrooms and Onions

This recipe is so simple but so exquisite. The steak seasons the vegetables while cooking, lending an earthy and salty flavor to the mushrooms and onions. The cooking time yields a medium-rare steak, so adjust for your preferred doneness.

- **Hands-On Time: 5 minutes**
- **Cook Time: 9 minutes**

Serves 2

1 tablespoon olive oil

8 ounces sliced white mushrooms

½ medium yellow onion, peeled and sliced into half-moons

⅛ teaspoon plus ½ teaspoon salt, divided

1 (¾-pound) strip steak

½ teaspoon smoked paprika

¼ teaspoon freshly ground black pepper

1 Preheat air fryer at 400°F for 3 minutes.

2 In a medium bowl, toss together olive oil, mushrooms, onion, and ⅛ teaspoon salt. Place in an even layer in ungreased air fryer basket.

3 Season steak with remaining ½ teaspoon salt, paprika, and pepper. Place steak on top of mushroom mixture.

4 Cook 5 minutes, then flip steak and cook an additional 4 minutes.

5 Transfer steak to a cutting board and let rest 5 minutes, then cut in half. Place steak, mushrooms, and onions on two large plates and serve warm.

PER SERVING

CALORIES: 311	FAT: 15g
PROTEIN: 37g	SODIUM: 803mg
FIBER: 2g	CARBOHYDRATES: 7g
NET CARBOHYDRATES: 5g	SUGAR: 3g

T-Bone with Garlic Rosemary Compound Butter

Compound butter is a just a fancy way to say butter with add-ins. If you've never experienced this little delicacy, start adding it to your steaks. It is so easy to make and lends so much flavor to your meal. You'll never go back!

- **Hands-On Time: 10 minutes**
- **Cook Time: 10 minutes**

Serves 2

2 tablespoons butter, softened

¼ teaspoon lemon juice

2 cloves garlic, peeled and minced

1 teaspoon minced fresh rosemary

1 (20-ounce, 1¼"-thick) T-bone steak, fat trimmed, leaving a ¼" ribbon

1 teaspoon salt

½ teaspoon freshly ground black pepper

2 tablespoons water

PRETTY COMPOUND BUTTER MOLDS

If you are wanting to display your butter in a better way than rolling it up in plastic wrap and forming a log, there are actual butter molds that can be purchased online. Alternatively, you can use silicone chocolate molds that come in all sorts of shapes and sizes and can be used for different celebrations!

1   Combine butter, lemon juice, garlic, and rosemary in a small bowl. Transfer butter onto parchment paper or plastic wrap. Roll into a log, spinning ends to tighten. Refrigerate 2 hours up to overnight.

2   Remove T-bone from refrigerator 30 minutes before cooking. Season with salt and pepper.

3   Preheat air fryer at 400°F for 3 minutes. Add 2 tablespoons water to air fryer.

4   Place steak in air fryer basket lightly greased with olive oil. Cook 5 minutes. Flip steak and cook an additional 5 minutes until a meat thermometer ensures an internal temperature of at least 135°F, or meat reaches desired doneness.

5   Transfer steak to a cutting board and let rest 5 minutes. Slice butter and add to top of steak. Let melt over meat. Serve warm.

PER SERVING

CALORIES: 627	FAT: 48g
PROTEIN: 45g	SODIUM: 1,276mg
FIBER: 0g	CARBOHYDRATES: 2g
NET CARBOHYDRATES: 1g	SUGAR: 0g

Greek Steak Bowls

The incredible spice blend and straight-out-of-the-air-fryer warmth of this steak plays nicely with the cooled nature of the vegetables and feta crumbles. In less than 15 minutes, you'll be dining exquisitely!

- **Hands-On Time: 5 minutes**
- **Cook Time: 9 minutes**

Serves 2

1 large English cucumber, diced

2 medium Roma tomatoes, cored, seeded, and diced

1 tablespoon apple cider vinegar

2 teaspoons olive oil

5 kalamata olives, pitted and halved

¼ cup feta cheese crumbles

½ teaspoon dried oregano

½ teaspoon dried dill

¼ teaspoon ground cinnamon

¼ teaspoon garlic powder

⅛ teaspoon ground nutmeg

½ teaspoon salt

¼ teaspoon freshly ground black pepper

1 (¾-pound) strip steak

1 Combine cucumber, tomatoes, apple cider vinegar, and olive oil in a medium bowl. Toss in olives and feta crumbles. Refrigerate covered until ready to use.

2 Preheat air fryer at 400°F for 3 minutes.

3 In a small bowl, combine oregano, dill, cinnamon, garlic powder, nutmeg, salt, and pepper. Season steak with mixture.

4 Place steak in air fryer basket lightly greased with olive oil. Cook 5 minutes, then flip steak and cook an additional 4 minutes or until desired doneness.

5 Transfer steak to a cutting board and let rest 5 minutes, then thinly slice against the grain and distribute between two medium bowls. Top with cucumber mixture and serve.

PER SERVING

CALORIES: 386	FAT: 20g
PROTEIN: 38g	SODIUM: 1,033mg
FIBER: 3g	CARBOHYDRATES: 14g
NET CARBOHYDRATES: 11g	SUGAR: 7g

Filet Mignon Steaks

There is nothing simple about filet mignon, so all you need is salt and pepper to let the natural flavors shine through. Don't forget to rest the meat before cutting, as this allows the juices to settle back into the meat rather than drip out onto the cutting board.

- **Hands-On Time:** 15 minutes
- **Cook Time:** 12 minutes

Serves 2

2 (8-ounce, 1½"-thick) filet mignon steaks
1 teaspoon salt
½ teaspoon freshly ground black pepper
1 tablespoon unsalted butter, cut into 2 pats

1 Preheat air fryer at 375°F for 3 minutes.

2 Season steaks on both sides with salt and pepper. Place in air fryer basket lightly greased with olive oil and cook 4 minutes. Flip and cook an additional 4 minutes. Flip one more time and cook an additional 4 minutes to yield a medium-rare steak.

3 Transfer steaks to a cutting board and top each with 1 pat butter. Let rest 5 minutes before serving.

PER SERVING

CALORIES: 369	FAT: 19g
PROTEIN: 46g	SODIUM: 1,258mg
FIBER: 0g	CARBOHYDRATES: 1g
NET CARBOHYDRATES: 0g	SUGAR: 0g

Flank Steak with Creamy Horseradish Sauce

Flank steak is one of the most underutilized cuts of beef because of its inexpensive nature, yet it rivals the tenderness of filet mignon if cut against the grain. The cool and creamy horseradish sauce adds a little kick to the steak.

- **Hands-On Time:** 10 minutes
- **Cook Time:** 9 minutes

Serves 2

For Creamy Horseradish Sauce
2 tablespoons prepared horseradish
2 tablespoons plain Greek yogurt
2 tablespoons mayonnaise
1 tablespoon fresh lemon juice
⅛ teaspoon salt
⅛ teaspoon freshly ground black pepper
½ teaspoon Worcestershire sauce

For Flank Steak
1 (12-ounce) flank steak, cut in half
2 tablespoons olive oil
1 teaspoon salt
½ teaspoon freshly ground black pepper

1 **To make Creamy Horseradish Sauce:** Whisk together all ingredients in a small bowl and refrigerate covered until ready to use.

2 **To make Flank Steak:** Preheat air fryer at 400°F for 3 minutes.

3 Rub flank steak halves with olive oil. Season with salt and pepper.

4 Place steaks in ungreased air fryer basket. Cook 4 minutes. Flip and cook an additional 5 minutes or until desired doneness.

5 Transfer steaks to a cutting board and let rest 5 minutes, then thinly slice against the grain and place on two medium plates.

6 Drizzle horseradish sauce over steaks and serve immediately.

PER SERVING

CALORIES: 480	FAT: 35g
PROTEIN: 36g	SODIUM: 1,547mg
FIBER: 1g	CARBOHYDRATES: 5g
NET CARBOHYDRATES: 4g	SUGAR: 2g

Peach Barbecue Pork Chops

Fruit pairs so nicely with pork chops, and this recipe won't let you down. The air fryer sears all sides of the chops while keeping the inside juicy! When choosing sugar-free jelly, read the labels, as some have hidden ingredients. Do a quick online search for "keto-accepted jelly" for a rundown of good options.

- **Hands-On Time:** 5 minutes
- **Cook Time:** 12 minutes

Serves 2

2 tablespoons sugar-free peach preserves

2 tablespoons no-sugar-added tomato paste

1 tablespoon Dijon mustard

1 teaspoon Worcestershire sauce

1 tablespoon fresh lemon juice

1 tablespoon olive oil

2 cloves garlic, peeled and minced

2 (1"-thick) bone-in pork chops

1 In a medium bowl, whisk together peach preserves, tomato paste, Dijon mustard, Worcestershire sauce, lemon juice, olive oil, and garlic. Add pork chops to mixture and toss. Refrigerate covered 30 minutes.

2 Preheat air fryer at 350°F for 3 minutes.

3 Place pork chops in ungreased air fryer basket. Cook 4 minutes. Flip and cook 4 more minutes. Flip once more and cook an additional 4 minutes. Using a meat thermometer, ensure internal temperature is at least 145°F.

4 Transfer pork to a cutting board and let rest 5 minutes before serving warm.

PER SERVING

CALORIES: 374	**FAT:** 22g
PROTEIN: 28g	**SODIUM:** 277mg
FIBER: 1g	**CARBOHYDRATES:** 18g
NET CARBOHYDRATES: 5g	**SUGAR:** 3g

Kickin' Mustard Parm Pork Chops

The *kickin'* in this recipe is from the horseradish mustard. If a little kick isn't what you like, simply use a Dijon or yellow mustard instead.

- **Hands-On Time: 5 minutes**
- **Cook Time: 12 minutes**

Serves 2

1 large egg white

1 tablespoon horseradish mustard

½ cup grated Parmesan cheese

¼ teaspoon freshly ground black pepper

2 (1"-thick) bone-in pork chops

¼ cup chopped fresh parsley

1 Preheat air fryer at 350°F for 3 minutes.

2 In a small dish, whisk together egg white and horseradish mustard. In a separate small shallow dish, combine Parmesan cheese and black pepper.

3 Dip pork chops in mustard mixture. Dredge in Parmesan mixture.

4 Place pork chops in air fryer basket lightly greased with olive oil. Cook 4 minutes. Flip and cook 4 minutes, then flip once more and cook an additional 4 minutes. Using a meat thermometer, ensure the internal temperature is at least 145°F.

5 Transfer pork to a cutting board and let rest 5 minutes before serving warm. Garnish with parsley.

PER SERVING

CALORIES: 474	**FAT:** 28g
PROTEIN: 51g	**SODIUM:** 543mg
FIBER: 1g	**CARBOHYDRATES:** 2g
NET CARBOHYDRATES: 1g	**SUGAR:** 0g

Carne Asada with Salsa Verde

Prep your Salsa Verde (see recipe in Chapter 3) ahead of time and marinate the meat the night before so you are ready to roll when you come home from a busy day. And it can be in your bowl in less than 25 minutes!

- **Hands-On Time: 10 minutes**
- **Cook Time: 11 minutes**

Serves 4

1 (2-pound) flank steak, cut in half

1½ cups Salsa Verde (see recipe in Chapter 3), divided

1 Place steaks in a large dish with 1 cup Salsa Verde. Cover and marinate refrigerated 1 hour up to overnight.

2 Preheat air fryer at 400°F for 3 minutes.

3 Place steaks in air fryer basket lightly greased with olive oil. Cook 6 minutes. Flip and cook an additional 5 minutes or until desired doneness.

4 Transfer steaks to a cutting board and let rest 5 minutes, then thinly slice against the grain and transfer to four medium plates. Serve warm with remaining ½ cup Salsa Verde.

PER SERVING

CALORIES: 326	**FAT:** 14g
PROTEIN: 46g	**SODIUM:** 165mg
FIBER: 1g	**CARBOHYDRATES:** 2g
NET CARBOHYDRATES: 2g	**SUGAR:** 1g

Chopped Steakhouse Salad

Although the plain walnuts lend an excellent crunch to this salad, try adding Candied Walnuts (see recipe in Chapter 9) for an extra boost of flavor.

- **Hands-On Time:** 10 minutes
- **Cook Time:** 9 minutes

Serves 2

2 tablespoons olive oil

1 tablespoon apple cider vinegar

1 tablespoon sour cream

1 teaspoon Dijon mustard

1 (¾-pound) strip steak

½ teaspoon salt

¼ teaspoon freshly ground black pepper

1 small head iceberg lettuce, cut into thin strips

2 tablespoons chopped walnuts

¼ cup blue cheese crumbles

4 medium cherry tomatoes, halved

¼ cup fresh blueberries

1 Whisk together olive oil, apple cider vinegar, sour cream, and Dijon mustard in a small bowl. Refrigerate covered until ready to use.

2 Preheat air fryer at 400°F for 3 minutes.

3 Season steak with salt and pepper. Place in air fryer basket lightly greased with olive oil. Cook 5 minutes, then flip and cook an additional 4 minutes or until desired doneness.

4 Transfer steak to a cutting board and let rest 5 minutes.

5 Transfer lettuce to a large serving bowl and toss with dressing, then transfer to two medium bowls.

6 Thinly slice steak and add to salads. Garnish with walnuts, blue cheese crumbles, tomatoes, and blueberries. Serve.

PER SERVING

CALORIES: 501	FAT: 32g
PROTEIN: 41g	SODIUM: 937mg
FIBER: 3g	CARBOHYDRATES: 12g
NET CARBOHYDRATES: 8g	SUGAR: 7g

Giant Italian Meatballs

What are better than meatballs? Giant meatballs! The ricotta and Parmesan cheeses lend a creaminess to the dish, while using beef and pork rounds out the flavor profile. And serving it in some marinara sauce...well, now, *that's* Italian!

- **Hands-On Time: 10 minutes**
- **Cook Time: 25 minutes**

Serves 4

- ½ pound 80/20 ground beef
- ½ pound ground pork
- 1 large egg, beaten
- 2 tablespoons no-sugar-added tomato paste
- ¼ cup ricotta cheese
- ⅓ cup grated Parmesan cheese
- 3 cloves garlic, peeled and minced
- ¼ cup peeled and grated yellow onion
- ½ teaspoon salt
- ¼ teaspoon freshly ground black pepper
- ¼ cup almond flour
- ¼ cup chopped fresh parsley
- 2 cups no-sugar-added marinara sauce

1 Combine all ingredients except for marinara sauce in a large bowl. Form mixture into four meatballs.

2 Preheat air fryer at 400°F for 3 minutes.

3 Cut a piece of parchment paper to fit bottom of air fryer basket. Place meatballs on paper. Cook 20 minutes.

4 In a medium skillet, heat sauce over medium heat 3 minutes. Add cooked meatballs and roll them around in sauce 2 minutes.

5 Transfer meatballs to a large plate and serve warm with sauce over the top.

PER SERVING

CALORIES: 399	FAT: 25g
PROTEIN: 29g	SODIUM: 732mg
FIBER: 3g	CARBOHYDRATES: 14g
NET CARBOHYDRATES: 10g	SUGAR: 7g

Juicy Beef Sliders

Who needs the bun when the meat is the star? The grated yellow onion lends a moistness to the beef, and no one in the family will even know you snuck it in! The simplicity of the seasoning adds just enough to let the burger shine.

- **Hands-On Time:** 5 minutes
- **Cook Time:** 18 minutes

Serves 4

1 pound 80/20 ground beef

⅓ cup peeled and grated yellow onion

½ teaspoon smoked paprika

½ teaspoon salt

¼ teaspoon freshly ground black pepper

1 In a medium bowl, combine all ingredients. Form into eight patties. Make a slight indentation in the middle of each.

2 Preheat air fryer at 350°F for 3 minutes.

3 Place four patties in air fryer basket or on air fryer grill pan lightly greased with olive oil. Cook 5 minutes. Flip sliders and cook an additional 4 minutes or until desired doneness.

4 Transfer cooked sliders to a large serving plate and repeat cooking with remaining sliders. Serve warm.

PER SERVING

CALORIES: 208	FAT: 13g
PROTEIN: 20g	SODIUM: 345mg
FIBER: 0g	CARBOHYDRATES: 1g
NET CARBOHYDRATES: 1g	SUGAR: 1g

Inside Out Barbecue Sliders

The cheese and bacon are *inside* the meat in this recipe, giving your guests a savory and cheesy surprise when they bite into these sliders. Change the flavor of the meat by trying different sugar-free barbecue sauces.

- **Hands-On Time: 5 minutes**
- **Cook Time: 18 minutes**

Yields 8 sliders

½ pound 80/20 ground beef

½ pound ground pork

1 tablespoon sugar-free barbecue sauce

½ teaspoon salt

¼ teaspoon freshly ground black pepper

4 slices sugar-free bacon, cooked and crumbled

8 (1-ounce) cubes Cheddar cheese

1 In a medium bowl, combine ground beef, ground pork, barbecue sauce, salt, and pepper. Form into eight equal balls.

2 Press your thumb into the center of each ball. Add bacon crumbles and Cheddar cheese cubes to hole. Seal.

3 Preheat air fryer at 350°F for 3 minutes.

4 Place four patties in air fryer basket or on air fryer grill pan lightly greased with olive oil. Cook 5 minutes. Flip sliders and cook an additional 4 minutes or until desired doneness.

5 Transfer cooked sliders to a large plate and repeat cooking with remaining sliders. Serve warm.

PER SERVING (1 SLIDER)

CALORIES: 241	**FAT:** 18g
PROTEIN: 18g	**SODIUM:** 444mg
FIBER: 0g	**CARBOHYDRATES:** 1g
NET CARBOHYDRATES: 1g	**SUGAR:** 1g

Dijon Rosemary Pork Loin Roast

This meal is simply seasoned to accent and allow the beautiful pork flavor to shine through. Because the loin roast is a less fatty cut, it is necessary to check the internal temperature toward the end of cooking. If overcooked, the roast can become dry. If cooked correctly, it is heaven!

- **Hands-On Time:** 10 minutes
- **Cook Time:** 40 minutes

Serves 4

2 tablespoons Dijon mustard
2 teaspoons olive oil
½ teaspoon salt
¼ teaspoon freshly ground black pepper
1 teaspoon dried rosemary
1 (2-pound) boneless pork loin roast

1 Preheat air fryer at 350°F for 3 minutes.

2 In a small bowl, whisk together mustard, olive oil, salt, pepper, and rosemary. Massage into loin on all sides.

3 Place pork in ungreased air fryer basket. Cook 20 minutes. Flip and cook an additional 20 minutes. Using a meat thermometer, ensure internal temperature is at least 145°F.

4 Transfer pork to a cutting board and let rest 5 minutes before slicing and serving warm.

PER SERVING

CALORIES: 423	FAT: 26g
PROTEIN: 42g	SODIUM: 546mg
FIBER: 0g	CARBOHYDRATES: 0g
NET CARBOHYDRATES: 0g	SUGAR: 0g

Blackened Pork Tenderloin

Here, *blackened* simply means that the meat has been dipped in butter and sprinkled with herbs and spices. The saltiness from the pork will enhance the other flavors as the air fryer crisps up the exterior.

- **Hands-On Time:** 10 minutes
- **Cook Time:** 16 minutes

Serves 2

1 tablespoon smoked paprika

2 teaspoons ground cumin

1 teaspoon garlic powder

1 teaspoon onion powder

¼ teaspoon cayenne pepper

1 teaspoon salt

½ teaspoon freshly ground black pepper

1 teaspoon Italian seasoning

2 tablespoons butter, melted

1 teaspoon Worcestershire sauce

1 (1-pound) pork tenderloin, halved crosswise

1 Combine paprika, cumin, garlic powder, onion powder, cayenne pepper, salt, black pepper, and Italian seasoning in a small bowl. Set aside.

2 Preheat air fryer at 350°F for 3 minutes.

3 Whisk together butter and Worcestershire sauce in a separate small bowl. Brush over pork tenderloin halves. Rub with seasoning mix.

4 Place pork in air fryer basket lightly greased with olive oil. Cook 8 minutes. Flip. Cook an additional 8 minutes. Using a meat thermometer, ensure internal temperature is at least 140°F.

5 Transfer pork to a cutting board and let rest 5 minutes before slicing and serving warm.

PER SERVING

CALORIES: 374	FAT: 18g
PROTEIN: 45g	SODIUM: 1,295mg
FIBER: 2g	CARBOHYDRATES: 6g
NET CARBOHYDRATES: 4g	SUGAR: 1g

Crispy Pork over Coconut Lime Cauliflower Rice

By thinly slicing the pork prior to cooking, you allow the air fryer to give this succulent meat those delicious crispy edges, which adds another dimension of flavor and texture to the dish.

- **Hands-On Time:** 15 minutes
- **Cook Time:** 25 minutes

Serves 4

For Pork
2 tablespoons avocado oil
2 tablespoons coconut aminos
2 teaspoons red chili paste
2 teaspoons yellow mustard
2 teaspoons granular erythritol
1 (1-pound) pork shoulder, trimmed and thinly sliced into 1" strips
2 tablespoons water

For Cauliflower Rice
1 tablespoon coconut oil
3 cups riced cauliflower
6 scallions, whites and greens separated, divided
4 cloves garlic, peeled and minced
1 cup canned unsweetened coconut milk
1 tablespoon fresh lime juice
1 teaspoon lime zest
½ teaspoon salt

1 **To make Pork:** In a medium bowl, whisk together avocado oil, coconut aminos, red chili paste, mustard, and erythritol. Set aside half of marinade. Add pork strips to bowl with remaining marinade and toss. Refrigerate pork covered 30 minutes.

2 Preheat air fryer at 350°F for 3 minutes. Pour water in bottom of air fryer to ensure minimum smoke from fat drippings.

3 Add pork to ungreased air fryer basket. Cook 7 minutes. Toss. Cook an additional 10 minutes.

4 Transfer pork to bowl with remaining marinade and toss. Set aside.

5 **To make Cauliflower Rice:** In a large skillet, heat coconut oil over medium-high heat 30 seconds. Add riced cauliflower, scallion whites, and garlic. Toss, then place lid on skillet, reduce heat to low, and let steam 2 minutes.

6 Uncover skillet and stir in coconut milk, lime juice, lime zest, and salt. Let cook uncovered an additional 5 minutes until heated through.

7 Serve pork over cauliflower rice and garnish with scallion greens.

PER SERVING

CALORIES: 338	**FAT:** 24g
PROTEIN: 20g	**SODIUM:** 664mg
FIBER: 2g	**CARBOHYDRATES:** 11g
NET CARBOHYDRATES: 7g	**SUGAR:** 4g

Dry-Rubbed Pork Ribs

The subtle dry rub used in this recipe is rich in flavors but tame enough for the entire family to enjoy. If you like a little heat, just add a pinch or two of cayenne pepper to the mix.

- **Hands-On Time: 10 minutes**
- **Cook Time: 40 minutes**

Serves 4

2 tablespoons water
1 teaspoon smoked paprika
1 teaspoon ground cumin
1 teaspoon garlic powder
1 tablespoon Swerve brown sugar
½ teaspoon ground mustard
1 teaspoon salt
½ teaspoon freshly ground black pepper
2 tablespoons olive oil
1 tablespoon fresh orange juice
2 pounds country-style pork ribs

1 Preheat air fryer at 350°F for 3 minutes. Pour water in bottom of air fryer to ensure minimum smoke from fat drippings.

2 In a small bowl, combine paprika, cumin, garlic powder, brown sugar, ground mustard, salt, and pepper. Set aside.

3 Whisk together olive oil and orange juice in a separate small bowl and massage into pork ribs. Season ribs with spice mixture.

4 Add pork to ungreased air fryer basket. Cook 40 minutes, flipping every 10 minutes.

5 Transfer pork to a large serving plate and serve warm.

PER SERVING

CALORIES: 464	FAT: 33g
PROTEIN: 39g	SODIUM: 667mg
FIBER: 1g	CARBOHYDRATES: 2g
NET CARBOHYDRATES: 1g	SUGAR: 0g

WHAT ARE COUNTRY-STYLE PORK RIBS?

Country-style pork ribs aren't actually cut from the ribs; they come from the end of the pork shoulder, which interestingly enough is also referred to as the *pork butt*! Regardless, these "ribs" are a boneless, delicious, fatty cut that is so, so very tender and worth a try. You'll come back for more!

Bratwursts, Onions, and Sauerkraut

If you would like to sub out the beef broth for beer when boiling the bratwurst, there are many low-carb beers available on the market. Just be sure to read labels, and enjoy a brew while the air fryer does its job!

- **Hands-On Time:** 10 minutes
- **Cook Time:** 21 minutes

Serves 4

1 pound (5 links) uncooked pork bratwurst, each piece pierced with a fork twice

2 cups beef broth

2 cups water

½ medium yellow onion, peeled and sliced into half-moons

2 cups drained sauerkraut

2 tablespoons German mustard

1   Add bratwurst, beef broth, water, and onion to a medium saucepan. Bring to a boil over high heat, then reduce heat to low and simmer 15 minutes. Drain.

2   Preheat air fryer at 400°F for 3 minutes.

3   Place bratwursts and onion in ungreased air fryer basket. Cook 3 minutes. Flip bratwursts, add sauerkraut, and cook an additional 3 minutes. Using a meat thermometer, ensure internal temperature is at least 160°F.

4   Transfer bratwursts, onion, and sauerkraut to a large serving plate and serve warm with mustard on the side.

PER SERVING

CALORIES: 240	FAT: 19g
PROTEIN: 11g	SODIUM: 1,537mg
FIBER: 2g	CARBOHYDRATES: 7g
NET CARBOHYDRATES: 4g	SUGAR: 2g

Mushroom Swiss–Stuffed Pork Loins

Mushrooms and Swiss cheese are just one of those magical combinations, like peanut butter and jelly. The pork loin is lean but still tender enough to lend some notes of rich fat to this tasty meal.

- **Hands-On Time:** 10 minutes
- **Cook Time:** 17 minutes

Serves 3

2 teaspoons olive oil

½ medium yellow onion, peeled and diced

¾ cup diced white mushrooms

½ teaspoon salt

½ teaspoon freshly ground black pepper

3 (1-pound, approximately 1"-thick) boneless center-cut pork loins, a pocket cut into each

6 thin slices Swiss cheese

1 In a medium skillet, heat olive oil over medium-high heat 2 minutes. Add onion and mushrooms and stir-fry 3 minutes until onion is translucent. Add salt and pepper. Continue to cook an additional minute.

2 Preheat air fryer at 350°F for 3 minutes.

3 Stuff an even amount of mushroom mixture into each pork chop pocket. Put 2 Swiss cheese slices into each pocket.

4 Place pork in air fryer basket lightly greased with olive oil. Cook 11 minutes. Using a meat thermometer, ensure internal temperature is at least 145°F.

5 Transfer pork to a cutting board and let rest 5 minutes before serving warm.

PER SERVING

CALORIES: 462		FAT: 31g	
PROTEIN: 39g		SODIUM: 509mg	
FIBER: 1g		CARBOHYDRATES: 3g	
NET CARBOHYDRATES: 2g		SUGAR: 1g	

Orange Ginger Pork Lettuce Wraps

This sweet and spicy pork is a perfect complement to healthy, low-carb lettuce wraps. If you have leftovers, try serving them over a bed of riced cauliflower or even atop a mixed green salad.

- **Hands-On Time: 15 minutes**
- **Cook Time: 20 minutes**

Serves 4

1 tablespoon arrowroot flour

1 tablespoon water

1 tablespoon apple cider vinegar

2 tablespoons sugar-free orange marmalade

1 teaspoon pulp-free orange juice

2 teaspoons sesame oil

⅛ teaspoon cayenne pepper

¼ teaspoon ground ginger

1 (1-pound) boneless pork loin, cut into 1" cubes

½ teaspoon salt

¼ teaspoon freshly ground white pepper

8 iceberg lettuce leaves

1 In a small bowl, create a slurry by whisking together arrowroot flour and water. Set aside.

2 In a small saucepan, combine apple cider vinegar, orange marmalade, orange juice, sesame oil, cayenne pepper, and ginger over medium heat. Cook 3 minutes, stirring continuously. Whisk in arrowroot slurry and heat another minute. Remove pan from heat and allow to thicken 3 minutes.

3 Preheat air fryer at 350°F for 3 minutes.

4 Season pork with salt and white pepper.

5 Add half of pork to air fryer basket lightly greased with olive oil. Cook 4 minutes. Shake gently. Cook an additional 4 minutes. Using a meat thermometer, ensure internal temperature is at least 145°F.

6 Transfer cooked pork to sauce. Repeat cooking with remaining pork, then add to sauce and toss. Serve warm in lettuce leaves.

PER SERVING

CALORIES: 258	FAT: 14g
PROTEIN: 22g	SODIUM: 335mg
FIBER: 2g	CARBOHYDRATES: 11g
NET CARBOHYDRATES: 3g	SUGAR: 2g

Banh Mi–Inspired Pork Bowl

A typical banh mi is a baguette sandwich filled with a Vietnamese-seasoned meat and pickled vegetables. This salad mimics those flavors, making it an addictive (and low-carb) bowl that you'll want to make over and over again!

- **Hands-On Time: 10 minutes**
- **Cook Time: 19 minutes**

Serves 4

For Crema
4 tablespoons sour cream
4 tablespoons mayonnaise
1 tablespoon fresh lime juice
½ teaspoon salt

For Vegetables
4 medium radishes, julienned
1 medium shallot, peeled and thinly sliced
3 tablespoons apple cider vinegar
⅛ teaspoon salt
2 medium carrots, peeled and shaved into ribbons
4 cups shredded napa cabbage
¼ cup chopped fresh basil
¼ cup chopped fresh mint

For Pork
1 tablespoon sesame oil
1 tablespoon coconut aminos
2 teaspoons red chili paste
2 teaspoons granular erythritol
1 (1") knob fresh ginger, peeled and minced
1 (1-pound) pork shoulder, trimmed and thinly sliced into 1" strips
2 tablespoons water

1. **To make Crema:** In a small bowl, whisk together ingredients. Refrigerate covered until ready to use.

2. **To make Vegetables:** In a medium bowl, add radishes, shallot, apple cider vinegar, and salt. Refrigerate covered until ready to use.

3. **To make Pork:** In a medium bowl, whisk together sesame oil, coconut aminos, red chili paste, erythritol, and ginger. Set aside half of marinade. Add pork strips to bowl with remaining marinade and toss. Refrigerate covered until ready to use.

4. Preheat air fryer at 350°F for 3 minutes. Pour water in bottom of air fryer to ensure minimum smoke from fat drippings.

5. Add pork to ungreased air fryer basket. Cook 5 minutes. Toss. Cook 6 minutes. Toss once more and cook an additional 6 minutes.

6. Transfer pork to bowl with remaining marinade and toss.

7. Add carrots to ungreased air fryer basket and cook 2 minutes.

8. **To assemble:** Distribute cabbage, basil, and mint in four medium bowls. Top with pork and vegetables. Drizzle crema over the top and serve.

PER SERVING

CALORIES: 383	**FAT:** 29g
PROTEIN: 20g	**SODIUM:** 740mg
FIBER: 2g	**CARBOHYDRATES:** 12g
NET CARBOHYDRATES: 8g	**SUGAR:** 5g

Juicy Pork Meatballs

Eat these meatballs right out of the air fryer, tossed in some warmed no-sugar-added marinara sauce or over a bed of steamed greens. The onion, yogurt, and cheese add a moistness that plays so nicely with the natural, juicy fattiness of ground pork. The almond flour and egg also help bind these meatballs together—you'll never miss the carb-filled bread crumbs!

- **Hands-On Time:** 15 minutes
- **Cook Time:** 16 minutes

Serves 4

1 pound ground pork
1 large egg
1 tablespoon plain Greek yogurt
¼ cup peeled and grated yellow onion
¼ cup finely chopped fresh parsley
¼ cup grated Parmesan cheese
2 tablespoons almond flour
¼ teaspoon garlic powder
¼ teaspoon salt
¼ teaspoon freshly ground black pepper

1 Preheat air fryer at 350°F for 3 minutes.

2 Combine all ingredients in a large bowl. Form into sixteen meatballs.

3 Add eight meatballs to air fryer basket lightly greased with olive oil and cook 6 minutes. Flip and cook an additional 2 minutes.

4 Transfer cooked meatballs to a large serving plate. Repeat cooking with remaining meatballs. Serve warm.

PER SERVING

CALORIES: 308
PROTEIN: 26g
FIBER: 1g
NET CARBOHYDRATES: 2g

FAT: 21g
SODIUM: 312mg
CARBOHYDRATES: 3g
SUGAR: 1g

Buffalo-Style Pork Meatballs

Whether it's game day or a Tuesday night after school, these low-carb buffalo-style meatballs will be at the top of everyone's list. Choose the heat via the sauce that you purchase, and don't forget to read those labels for any hidden ingredients!

- **Hands-On Time: 15 minutes**
- **Cook Time: 16 minutes**

Serves 4

1 pound ground pork
1 large egg
¼ cup buffalo wing sauce
¼ cup grated celery
¼ cup finely chopped fresh
    parsley
¼ cup almond flour
¼ teaspoon salt

HOMEMADE BLUE CHEESE DRESSING

So simple, so fresh! Combine the following ingredients for some homemade blue cheese dressing: ½ cup mayonnaise, ¼ cup sour cream, 2 teaspoons whole milk or cream, 1 teaspoon lemon juice, 1 peeled and minced clove garlic, ¼ teaspoon salt, ¼ teaspoon freshly ground black pepper, ⅓ cup blue cheese crumbles, and 2 tablespoons chopped fresh chives. Cover with a lid and refrigerate for up to five days.

1 Preheat air fryer at 350°F for 3 minutes.

2 Combine all ingredients in a large bowl. Form into sixteen meatballs.

3 Add eight meatballs to air fryer basket lightly greased with olive oil and cook 6 minutes. Flip and cook an additional 2 minutes.

4 Transfer cooked meatballs to a large serving plate. Repeat cooking with remaining meatballs. Serve warm.

PER SERVING

CALORIES: 303		FAT: 22g	
PROTEIN: 24g		SODIUM: 583mg	
FIBER: 1g		CARBOHYDRATES: 2g	
NET CARBOHYDRATES: 1g		SUGAR: 1g	

7

Fish and Seafood Main Dishes

Seafood is one of those meals that you may order a lot at restaurants but overlook at home. A terrific source of protein and other nutrients—not to mention low in carbs *and* calories—it is a fare worth embracing in your kitchen. A lot of home chefs are timid when it comes to cooking fish and shellfish, but it's time to conquer those fears: They make some of the quickest meals you can cook in your air fryer! The air fryer yields a crisp topping on a juicy fillet. In addition, your fried oyster, shrimp, fish stick, and even calamari favorites can be enjoyed without the fatty cooking oil and carbs in traditional deep-fried foods.

From Crab-Stuffed Mushrooms to Breaded Fish Sticks with Tartar Sauce and Tuna Croquettes, this chapter covers a variety of delicious fish and shellfish recipes that will have you eating seafood on a regular basis.

Crab-Stuffed Mushrooms

As a full meal, side dish, or appetizer, these scrumptious and creamy Crab-Stuffed Mushrooms have a nice crunch from the bread crumb topping made crisp in the air fryer.

- **Hands-On Time:** 10 minutes
- **Cook Time:** 20 minutes

Serves 6

2 ounces cream cheese, at room temperature

½ cup lump crabmeat, shells discarded

1 teaspoon prepared horseradish

1 teaspoon lemon juice

½ teaspoon salt

½ teaspoon freshly ground black pepper

16 ounces baby bella (cremini) mushrooms, stems removed

2 tablespoons panko bread crumbs

2 tablespoons butter, melted

¼ cup chopped fresh parsley

1 In a medium bowl, combine cream cheese, crabmeat, horseradish, lemon juice, salt, and pepper.

2 Preheat air fryer at 350°F for 5 minutes.

3 Evenly stuff cream cheese mixture into mushroom caps. Distribute bread crumbs over stuffed mushrooms. Drizzle melted butter over bread crumbs.

4 Place half of mushrooms in fryer basket. Cook 10 minutes. Transfer to serving plate. Repeat with remaining mushrooms.

5 Garnish with chopped parsley. Serve warm.

PER SERVING

CALORIES: 99	**FAT:** 7g
PROTEIN: 5g	**SODIUM:** 274mg
FIBER: 1g	**CARBOHYDRATES:** 5g
NET CARBOHYDRATES: 4g	**SUGAR:** 2g

Oysters Rockefeller

Fresh oysters can be found in the fresh seafood section of most grocers. If you are not game to shuck the oysters yourself, ask your fishmonger. This is generally a task that they will provide at no additional cost. Tell them to save the shells, though, so you can make this delicious Oysters Rockefeller!

- **Hands-On Time:** 10 minutes
- **Cook Time:** 16 minutes

Serves 2

2 tablespoons butter

1 medium shallot, peeled and minced

1 clove garlic, peeled and minced

1 cup chopped fresh baby spinach

4 teaspoons grated Parmesan cheese

⅛ teaspoon Tabasco original hot sauce

½ teaspoon fresh lemon juice

¼ cup crushed garlic pork rinds

12 oysters, on the half shell, rinsed and patted dry

1 In a small skillet, heat butter over medium heat 30 seconds. Add shallot, garlic, and spinach. Stir-fry 3 minutes until shallot is translucent.

2 Add Parmesan cheese, Tabasco sauce, lemon juice, and pork rinds to skillet. Distribute mixture to tops of oysters.

3 Preheat air fryer at 400°F for 3 minutes.

4 Place half of oysters in ungreased air fryer basket. Cook 6 minutes.

5 Transfer cooked oysters to a large serving plate and repeat cooking with remaining oysters. Serve warm.

PER SERVING

CALORIES: 198	FAT: 15g
PROTEIN: 9g	SODIUM: 213mg
FIBER: 1g	CARBOHYDRATES: 6g
NET CARBOHYDRATES: 5g	SUGAR: 2g

Steamer Clams

Littleneck clams are not only inexpensive, but they are also a lean source of protein with few carbs. Eat them alone or with some zoodles (zucchini noodles).

- **Hands-On Time: 20 minutes**
- **Cook Time: 7 minutes**

Serves 2

25 littleneck clams, scrubbed
2 tablespoons water
2 tablespoons butter, melted
2 lemon wedges

1 Place clams in a large bowl filled with water. Let stand 10 minutes. Drain. Refill bowl with water and let stand an additional 10 minutes. Drain.

2 Preheat air fryer at 350°F for 3 minutes.

3 Pour 2 tablespoons water into bottom of air fryer. Add clams to ungreased air fryer basket. Cook 7 minutes. Discard any clams that don't open.

4 Remove clams from shells and add to a large serving dish with melted butter. Squeeze lemon on top and serve.

PER SERVING

CALORIES: 279	FAT: 14g
PROTEIN: 30g	SODIUM: 1,429mg
FIBER: 0g	CARBOHYDRATES: 7g
NET CARBOHYDRATES: 7g	SUGAR: 0g

Bay Scallops

Cook these to enjoy as the main protein in your meal or as a topping in your favorite salad.

- **Hands-On Time: 5 minutes**
- **Cook Time: 5 minutes**

Serves 4

2 tablespoons butter, melted
Juice from 1 medium lime
¼ teaspoon salt
1 pound bay scallops

1 Preheat air fryer at 350°F for 3 minutes.

2 In a medium bowl, whisk together butter, lime juice, and salt. Add scallops and toss.

3 Place scallops in ungreased air fryer basket. Cook 2 minutes. Toss scallops. Cook an additional 3 minutes.

4 Transfer scallops to a serving dish. Serve warm.

PER SERVING

CALORIES: 132	FAT: 6g
PROTEIN: 14g	SODIUM: 591mg
FIBER: 0g	CARBOHYDRATES: 4g
NET CARBOHYDRATES: 4g	SUGAR: 0g

Smoky Fried Calamari

Calamari can be found in the frozen section, sometimes already cut into circles; however, fresh squid tubes can be purchased at the fish counter, and they are easy to slice at home.

- **Hands-On Time:** 15 minutes
- **Cook Time:** 8 minutes

Serves 4

2 tablespoons no-sugar-added tomato paste

1 tablespoon gochujang

1 tablespoon fresh lime juice

1 teaspoon smoked paprika

½ teaspoon salt

1 cup crushed pork rinds

⅓ pound (about 6) calamari tubes, cut into ¼" rings

1   Preheat air fryer at 400°F for 3 minutes.

2   In a medium bowl, whisk together tomato paste, gochujang, lime juice, paprika, and salt. Add pork rinds to a separate shallow dish.

3   Dredge a calamari ring in tomato mixture. Shake off excess. Roll through pork rind crumbs. Repeat with remaining rings.

4   Place half of calamari rings in air fryer basket lightly greased with olive oil. Cook 2 minutes. Gently flip and cook an additional 2 minutes.

5   Transfer cooked calamari to a large serving dish and repeat cooking with remaining calamari. Serve warm.

PER SERVING

CALORIES: 99

PROTEIN: 11g

FIBER: 1g

NET CARBOHYDRATES: 5g

FAT: 3g

SODIUM: 545mg

CARBOHYDRATES: 6g

SUGAR: 2g

Breaded Fish Sticks with Tartar Sauce

Cook these low-carb fish sticks for your kids, or just for yourself to bring back some childhood memories. Cod is used in this recipe, but any firm whitefish works. You can even get experimental and try your hand at salmon sticks!

- **Hands-On Time:** 10 minutes
- **Cook Time:** 20 minutes

Serves 4

For Tartar Sauce
½ cup mayonnaise
1 tablespoon Dijon mustard
½ cup small-diced dill pickles
⅛ teaspoon salt
¼ teaspoon freshly ground black pepper

For Fish Sticks
1 large egg, beaten
¼ cup arrowroot flour
¼ cup almond flour
½ teaspoon salt
¼ teaspoon freshly ground black pepper
1 pound cod, cut into 1" sticks

1 **To make Tartar Sauce:** Combine all ingredients in a small bowl and refrigerate covered until ready to use.

2 **To make Fish Sticks:** Preheat air fryer at 350°F for 3 minutes.

3 Place egg in a small bowl. Combine arrowroot flour, almond flour, salt, and pepper in a separate shallow dish.

4 Dip a fish stick in egg. Shake off excess egg. Roll in flour mixture. Transfer to a large plate. Repeat with remaining fish sticks.

5 Place half of fish sticks in air fryer basket lightly greased with olive oil. Cook 5 minutes. Carefully flip fish sticks. Cook an additional 5 minutes.

6 Transfer cooked fish sticks to a large serving plate and repeat cooking with remaining fish sticks. Serve warm with tartar sauce on the side.

PER SERVING

CALORIES: 363	**FAT:** 26g
PROTEIN: 21g	**SODIUM:** 855mg
FIBER: 1g	**CARBOHYDRATES:** 9g
NET CARBOHYDRATES: 8g	**SUGAR:** 1g

Crab Cakes with Arugula and Blackberry Salad

This is a simple yet elegant lunch filled with nutrients and flavor. You'll never know that the traditional carb-filled bread crumbs aren't in these crab cakes, as the sweet taste of the crab will shine through.

- **Hands-On Time:** 15 minutes
- **Cook Time:** 10 minutes

Serves 2

For Crab Cakes
8 ounces lump crabmeat, shells discarded
2 tablespoons mayonnaise
½ teaspoon Dijon mustard
½ teaspoon lemon juice
2 teaspoons peeled and minced yellow onion
¼ teaspoon prepared horseradish
¼ cup almond meal
1 large egg white, beaten
½ teaspoon Old Bay Seasoning

For Salad
1 tablespoon olive oil
2 teaspoons lemon juice
⅛ teaspoon salt
⅛ teaspoon freshly ground black pepper
4 ounces fresh arugula
½ cup fresh blackberries
¼ cup walnut pieces
2 lemon wedges

1 **To make Crab Cakes:** Preheat air fryer at 400°F for 3 minutes.

2 In a medium bowl, combine all ingredients. Form into four patties.

3 Place patties into air fryer basket lightly greased with olive oil. Cook 5 minutes. Flip patties. Cook an additional 5 minutes.

4 Transfer crab cakes to a large plate. Set aside.

5 **To make Salad:** In a large bowl, whisk together olive oil, lemon juice, salt, and pepper. Add arugula and toss. Distribute into two medium bowls.

6 Add two crab cakes to each bowl. Garnish with blackberries, walnuts, and lemon wedges. Serve.

PER SERVING

CALORIES: 406		**FAT:** 29g	
PROTEIN: 29g		**SODIUM:** 790mg	
FIBER: 4g		**CARBOHYDRATES:** 10g	
NET CARBOHYDRATES: 6g		**SUGAR:** 4g	

Bacon-Wrapped Stuffed Shrimp

Shrimp stuffed with cheese and wrapped in bacon is an irresistible combination. Make sure you buy the large shrimp for this recipe. The bacon takes longer to cook than small shrimp, so the end result is better with larger shrimp.

- **Hands-On Time: 10 minutes**
- **Cook Time: 18 minutes**

Serves 4

1 pound (about 20) large raw shrimp, deveined and shelled

3 tablespoons crumbled goat cheese

2 tablespoons panko bread crumbs

¼ teaspoon Worcestershire sauce

½ teaspoon prepared horseradish

¼ teaspoon garlic powder

2 teaspoons mayonnaise

¼ teaspoon freshly ground black pepper

2 tablespoons water

5 slices bacon, quartered

¼ cup chopped fresh parsley

1 Butterfly shrimp by cutting down the spine of each shrimp without going all the way through.

2 In a medium bowl, combine goat cheese, bread crumbs, Worcestershire sauce, horse-radish, garlic powder, mayonnaise, and pepper.

3 Preheat air fryer at 400°F for 3 minutes. Pour 2 tablespoons water into bottom of air fryer.

4 Evenly press goat cheese mixture into shrimp. Wrap a piece of bacon around each piece of shrimp to hold in cheese mixture.

5 Place half of shrimp in fryer basket. Cook 5 minutes. Flip shrimp. Cook an additional 4 minutes. Transfer to serving plate. Repeat with remaining shrimp.

6 Garnish with chopped parsley. Serve warm.

PER SERVING

CALORIES: 174		**FAT:** 8g
PROTEIN: 20g		**SODIUM:** 833mg
FIBER: 0g		**CARBOHYDRATES:** 4g
NET CARBOHYDRATES: 3g		**SUGAR:** 0g

Simply Shrimp

Shrimp are not only high in protein, but they are also delicious and low in calories. Eat them plain, in a salad, over cauliflower "grits," warm, chilled, or dipped! They are such a versatile and fairly inexpensive protein, and they can be made in a snap using your air fryer.

- **Hands-On Time: 5 minutes**
- **Cook Time: 6 minutes**

Serves 2

1 pound medium raw shrimp, tail on, deveined, and thawed or fresh
2 tablespoons butter, melted
1 tablespoon fresh lemon juice (about ½ medium lemon)

1 Preheat air fryer at 350°F for 3 minutes.

2 In a large bowl, toss shrimp in butter.

3 Place shrimp in air fryer basket lightly greased with olive oil. Cook 4 minutes. Gently flip shrimp. Cook an additional 2 minutes.

4 Transfer shrimp to a large serving plate. Squeeze lemon juice over shrimp and serve.

PER SERVING

CALORIES: 265	FAT: 14g
PROTEIN: 31g	SODIUM: 1,285mg
FIBER: 0g	CARBOHYDRATES: 3g
NET CARBOHYDRATES: 3g	SUGAR: 0g

Chili Lime–Crusted Halibut

Pork rinds are such a great way to get in a little crunch without any of the carb-filled grain. Bread this halibut with different flavors of pork rinds for more variety.

- **Hands-On Time: 10 minutes**
- **Cook Time: 10 minutes**

Serves 2

2 tablespoons butter, melted
½ cup crushed chili lime–flavored pork rinds
2 (6-ounce) halibut fillets

1 Preheat air fryer at 350°F for 3 minutes.

2 Combine butter and pork rinds in a small bowl. Press mixture onto tops of halibut fillets.

3 Place fish in air fryer basket lightly greased with olive oil. Cook 10 minutes until fish is opaque and flakes easily with a fork.

4 Transfer fish to two medium plates and serve warm.

PER SERVING

CALORIES: 269	FAT: 15g
PROTEIN: 32g	SODIUM: 239mg
FIBER: 0g	CARBOHYDRATES: 0g
NET CARBOHYDRATES: 0g	SUGAR: 0g

Tuna Croquettes

Traditionally, croquettes are a fried delicacy; the word *croquette* comes from the French word *croquer*, which literally means "crunch." However, with the air fryer, you'll get all the crispness without the deep-fried fat and carbs. Also, don't discard your celery leaves: Chop them up and serve them over your croquettes, or add them to a salad at a later date!

- **Hands-On Time:** 15 minutes
- **Cook Time:** 24 minutes

Serves 4

1 (12-ounce) can tuna in water, drained

⅓ cup mayonnaise

1 tablespoon minced fresh celery

2 teaspoons dried dill, divided

1 teaspoon fresh lime juice

1 cup crushed pork rinds, divided

1 large egg

1 teaspoon prepared horseradish

1 Preheat air fryer at 375°F for 3 minutes.

2 In a medium bowl, combine tuna, mayonnaise, celery, 1 teaspoon dill, lime juice, ¼ cup pork rinds, egg, and horseradish.

3 Form mixture into twelve rectangular mound shapes (about 2 tablespoons each). Roll each croquette in a shallow dish with remaining crushed pork rinds.

4 Place six croquettes in air fryer basket lightly greased with olive oil. Cook 4 minutes. Gently turn one third. Cook an additional 4 minutes. Gently turn another third. Cook an additional 4 minutes.

5 Transfer cooked croquettes to a large serving dish. Repeat cooking with remaining croquettes and garnish with remaining dill. Serve warm.

PER SERVING

CALORIES: 241	FAT: 18g
PROTEIN: 19g	SODIUM: 440mg
FIBER: 0g	CARBOHYDRATES: 0g
NET CARBOHYDRATES: 0g	SUGAR: 0g

Buttery Lobster Tails

Whether you are cooking them to eat as a main course, chopped into a lettuce wrap, or sliced atop a salad, these Buttery Lobster Tails are a luxurious low-carb, low-calorie protein that is sure to please!

- **Hands-On Time: 10 minutes**
- **Cook Time: 8 minutes**

Serves 2

2 (6-ounce) uncooked lobster tails, thawed

1 tablespoon butter, melted

½ teaspoon Old Bay Seasoning

1 tablespoon chopped fresh parsley

2 lemon wedges

MAKING BROTH WITH LOBSTER TAIL SHELLS

Don't discard those empty lobster tail shells, as they can be used for a beautiful broth for lobster bisque, crab soup, or seafood gumbo. Place the shells in a Dutch oven or heavy-bottomed pot with 4 cups water, 1 medium peeled and diced yellow onion, 1 medium peeled and diced carrot, 1 diced stalk celery, and 2 peeled and halved cloves garlic. Bring to a boil over high heat. Reduce heat and simmer covered 30 minutes. Use a slotted spoon to remove and discard the solids from the broth. Strain the remaining liquid through a fine-mesh sieve or cheesecloth. Refrigerate covered up to four days or freeze up to six months.

1 Preheat air fryer at 400°F for 3 minutes.

2 Using kitchen shears, cut down the middle of each lobster tail on the softer side. Carefully run your finger between the lobster meat and the shell to loosen meat.

3 Place lobster tails in ungreased air fryer basket, cut sides up. Cook 4 minutes. Brush with butter and sprinkle with Old Bay Seasoning. Cook an additional 4 minutes.

4 Serve warm, garnished with parsley and lemon wedges.

PER SERVING

CALORIES: 154	FAT: 7g
PROTEIN: 21g	SODIUM: 889mg
FIBER: 0g	CARBOHYDRATES: 1g
NET CARBOHYDRATES: 1g	SUGAR: 0g

Tuna Melts on Tomatoes

Put aside those carb-filled English muffins: Tuna salad doesn't need them anymore! Choose ripe red tomatoes for slices that will be the base for this tasty meal.

- **Hands-On Time: 10 minutes**
- **Cook Time: 4 minutes**

Serves 2

1 (6-ounce) can tuna in water, drained

¼ cup mayonnaise

2 teaspoons yellow mustard

1 tablespoon minced dill pickle

1 tablespoon minced celery

1 tablespoon peeled and minced yellow onion

⅛ teaspoon salt

⅛ teaspoon freshly ground black pepper

4 thick slices large beefsteak tomato

1 small avocado, peeled, pitted, and cut into 8 slices

½ cup grated mild Cheddar cheese

1 Combine tuna, mayonnaise, mustard, pickles, celery, onion, salt, and pepper in a medium bowl.

2 Preheat air fryer at 350°F for 3 minutes.

3 Cut a piece of parchment paper to fit the bottom of the air fryer basket. Place tomato slices on paper in single layer. Place two avocado slices on each tomato slice. Distribute tuna salad over avocado slices. Top evenly with cheese.

4 Place stacks in ungreased air fryer basket and cook 4 minutes until cheese starts to brown. Serve warm.

PER SERVING

CALORIES: 532	FAT: 46g
PROTEIN: 22g	SODIUM: 762mg
FIBER: 8g	CARBOHYDRATES: 13g
NET CARBOHYDRATES: 5g	SUGAR: 3g

Classic Lobster Salad

This luscious salad pairs perfectly with a glass of dry white wine or chilled rosé. The tarragon can be switched out for dill, and if you have only a lime on hand, use it instead of the lemon. Always remember that you can tailor recipes to your taste buds (or the ingredients in your refrigerator). Have fun, and make it your own recipe!

- **Hands-On Time: 10 minutes**
- **Cook Time: 8 minutes**

Serves 2

2 (6-ounce) uncooked lobster tails, thawed

¼ cup mayonnaise

2 teaspoons fresh lemon juice

1 small stalk celery, sliced

2 teaspoons chopped fresh chives

2 teaspoons chopped fresh tarragon

¼ teaspoon salt

⅛ teaspoon freshly ground black pepper

2 thick slices large beefsteak tomato

1 small avocado, peeled, pitted, and diced

1 Preheat air fryer at 400°F for 3 minutes.

2 Using kitchen shears, cut down the middle of each lobster tail on the softer side. Carefully run your finger between the lobster meat and the shell to loosen meat.

3 Place lobster tails, cut sides up, in ungreased air fryer basket. Cook 8 minutes.

4 Transfer tails to a large plate and let cool about 3 minutes until easy to handle, then pull lobster meat from shell. Roughly chop meat and add to a medium bowl.

5 Add mayonnaise, lemon juice, celery, chives, tarragon, salt, and pepper to bowl. Combine.

6 Divide lobster salad between two medium plates, top with tomato slices, and garnish with avocado. Serve.

PER SERVING

CALORIES: 463		FAT: 36g
PROTEIN: 24g		SODIUM: 1,343mg
FIBER: 7g		CARBOHYDRATES: 12g
NET CARBOHYDRATES: 5g		SUGAR: 3g

Baked Avocados with Smoked Salmon

This meal is exploding with flavors and nutrients. Air frying avocados not only heats them up but also softens the flesh. The caper and cream cheese mixture also lends a smooth and salty topping that pairs perfectly with the salmon. You won't believe it's low-carb!

- **Hands-On Time:** 10 minutes
- **Cook Time:** 8 minutes

Serves 2

¼ cup apple cider vinegar

1 teaspoon granular erythritol

¼ cup peeled and sliced red onion

2 ounces cream cheese, room temperature

1 tablespoon capers, drained

2 large avocados, peeled, halved, and pitted

4 ounces smoked salmon

2 medium cherry tomatoes, halved

1 In a small saucepan, heat apple cider vinegar and erythritol over high heat 4 minutes until boiling. Add onion and remove saucepan from heat. Let set while preparing remaining ingredients. Drain when ready to use onions.

2 Combine cream cheese and capers in a small bowl. Cover and refrigerate until ready to use.

3 Preheat air fryer at 350°F for 3 minutes.

4 Place avocado halves, cut sides up, in ungreased air fryer basket and cook 4 minutes.

5 Transfer avocados to two medium plates and garnish with cream cheese mixture, smoked salmon, pickled onions, and tomato halves. Serve.

PER SERVING

CALORIES: 501	FAT: 42g
PROTEIN: 16g	SODIUM: 590mg
FIBER: 14g	CARBOHYDRATES: 22g
NET CARBOHYDRATES: 6g	SUGAR: 3g

Salmon Cakes with Lemon Caper Sauce

This recipe calls for canned salmon for ease; however, leftover or freshly cooked salmon flaked into pieces are both great options for these powerhouse patties with omega-3 fatty acids.

- **Hands-On Time:** 10 minutes
- **Cook Time:** 20 minutes

Serves 4

For Lemon Caper Sauce
¼ cup sour cream
2 tablespoons mayonnaise
2 cloves garlic, peeled and minced
¼ teaspoon caper juice
2 teaspoons lemon juice

For Salmon Patties
1 (14.75-ounce) can salmon, drained
½ cup mayonnaise
2 teaspoons lemon zest
1 large egg
2 tablespoons seeded and finely minced red bell pepper
½ cup almond meal
⅛ teaspoon salt
2 tablespoons capers, drained

1 **To make Lemon Caper Sauce:** In a small bowl, combine sour cream, mayonnaise, garlic, caper juice, and lemon juice. Refrigerate covered until ready to use.

2 **To make Salmon Patties:** Preheat air fryer at 400°F for 3 minutes.

3 In a medium bowl, combine salmon, mayonnaise, lemon zest, egg, bell pepper, almond meal, and salt. Form into eight patties.

4 Place four patties in air fryer basket lightly greased with olive oil. Cook 5 minutes. Gently flip and cook an additional 5 minutes.

5 Transfer cooked patties to a large serving dish and repeat cooking with remaining patties. Let rest 5 minutes, then drizzle with lemon caper sauce and garnish with capers. Serve.

PER SERVING

CALORIES: 471	**FAT:** 41g
PROTEIN: 21g	**SODIUM:** 832mg
FIBER: 2g	**CARBOHYDRATES:** 5g
NET CARBOHYDRATES: 3g	**SUGAR:** 1g

Seared Sea Scallops

The convection oven-style of cooking in the air fryer sears these scallops beautifully on all sides. Serve the scallops with steamed asparagus, mashed potatoes, and a drizzle of fresh hollandaise sauce over everything for decadent bites of yummy!

- **Hands-On Time: 5 minutes**
- **Cook Time: 8 minutes**

Serves 2

2 tablespoons butter, melted

1 tablespoon fresh lemon juice

1 pound (about 10) jumbo sea scallops

1 Preheat air fryer at 400°F for 3 minutes.

2 In a small bowl, combine butter and lemon juice. Roll scallops in mixture to coat all sides.

3 Place scallops in ungreased air fryer basket. Cook 2 minutes. Flip scallops. Cook 2 minutes more. Brush the tops of each scallop with butter mixture. Cook 2 minutes. Flip scallops. Cook an additional 2 minutes.

4 Transfer scallops to a large serving plate and serve warm.

PER SERVING

CALORIES: 260	FAT: 13g
PROTEIN: 27g	SODIUM: 891mg
FIBER: 0g	CARBOHYDRATES: 8g
NET CARBOHYDRATES: 8g	SUGAR: 0g

Dijon Pork Panko-Crusted Cod

Pork Panko is another name for crushed pork rinds, because they are used in place of the Panko bread crumbs traditionally used in breading. The pork rinds lend a crunchiness and a "bready" quality—without the carbs. You can find pork rinds in a variety of flavors, so don't be afraid to experiment or to even make your own by crushing your own pork rinds.

- **Hands-On Time:** 10 minutes
- **Cook Time:** 10 minutes

Serves 2

½ cup crushed pork rinds
⅛ teaspoon salt
1 tablespoon Dijon mustard
1 teaspoon fresh lemon juice
1 tablespoon butter, melted
2 (6-ounce) cod fillets

1 Preheat air fryer at 350°F for 3 minutes.

2 In a small bowl, combine pork rinds, salt, mustard, lemon juice, and butter. Press mixture evenly across tops of cod fillets. Place cod in air fryer basket lightly greased with olive oil.

3 Cook cod 10 minutes until opaque and flakes easily with a fork.

4 Transfer fillets to two medium plates and serve warm.

PER SERVING

CALORIES: 226
PROTEIN: 32g
FIBER: 0g
NET CARBOHYDRATES: 0g

FAT: 9g
SODIUM: 563mg
CARBOHYDRATES: 0g
SUGAR: 0g

Fried Sardines with Romesco Dipping Sauce

Sardines can have a bad reputation, but seriously, they taste amazing and are packed with omega-3s, vitamin D, protein, and selenium. And as a bonus, they are economical and low in mercury and other metals commonly found in fish. Paired with the low-carb romesco sauce, this is one delicious meal!

- **Hands-On Time: 5 minutes**
- **Cook Time: 6 minutes**

Serves 2

½ cup crushed pork rinds

2 (3.75-ounce) cans skinless, boneless sardines packed in oil, drained

½ cup warmed romesco sauce

1 Preheat air fryer at 350°F for 3 minutes.

2 Place ground pork rinds in a shallow dish. Roll sardines to coat with ground pork rinds.

3 Place coated sardines in air fryer basket lightly greased with olive oil. Cook 3 minutes. Gently flip sardines and cook an additional 3 minutes.

4 Transfer to a medium serving dish and serve warm with romesco sauce.

PER SERVING

CALORIES: 441	**FAT:** 36g
PROTEIN: 23g	**SODIUM:** 836mg
FIBER: 3g	**CARBOHYDRATES:** 4g
NET CARBOHYDRATES: 1g	**SUGAR:** 1g

HOW TO MAKE A QUICK AND EASY ROMESCO SAUCE

Heat the following ingredients in a medium saucepan over medium-high heat for 5 minutes: 1 (12-ounce) jar drained roasted red peppers, ½ cup canned drained diced tomatoes, ½ cup chopped fresh parsley, 2 peeled and halved cloves garlic, ½ cup chopped almonds, ¼ cup olive oil, 1 tablespoon cooking sherry, ½ teaspoon smoked paprika, ¼ teaspoon cayenne pepper, ½ teaspoon salt, and ¼ teaspoon freshly ground black pepper. Transfer to a blender and blend until smooth. Pour sauce into a lidded container and refrigerate up to five days. Yields approximately 2 cups.

Pesto Tilapia Roulade

Tilapia is a mild whitefish that is the perfect vessel for the fresh and bright flavors of pesto. Topping the roulade with crushed cornflakes adds a layer of texture, making these simple ingredients shine.

- **Hands-On Time: 15 minutes**
- **Cook Time: 6 minutes**

Serves 4

4 (5-ounce) tilapia fillets
1 large egg
2 tablespoons water
1 cup crushed cornflakes
1 teaspoon salt
½ teaspoon freshly ground
   black pepper
4 teaspoons pesto
2 tablespoons butter, melted
4 lime wedges

1 Between two pieces of parchment paper, gently pound tilapia fillets until "rollable," about ¼" thickness.

2 In a small bowl, whisk together egg and water.

3 In a shallow dish, combine cornflakes, salt, and pepper.

4 Preheat air fryer at 350°F for 3 minutes.

5 Spread 1 teaspoon pesto on each fish fillet. Tightly and gently roll a fillet from one short end to the other. Secure with a toothpick. Repeat with each fillet.

6 Roll each fillet in egg mixture and dredge in cornflake mixture.

7 Place fish in lightly greased air fryer basket. Drizzle tops with melted butter. Cook 6 minutes.

8 Transfer to a serving dish and let rest 5 minutes. Remove toothpicks. Serve warm with lime wedges.

PER SERVING

CALORIES: 173	FAT: 10g
PROTEIN: 16g	SODIUM: 576mg
FIBER: 1g	CARBOHYDRATES: 5g
NET CARBOHYDRATES: 5g	SUGAR: 1g

Cajun Cod with Shrimp Mango Salsa

The heat from the Cajun seasoning is tempered by the soothing mango, tomatoes, and shrimp in this decadent salsa.

- **Hands-On Time:** 10 minutes
- **Cook Time:** 10 minutes

Serves 2

For Shrimp Mango Salsa
¼ cup chopped cooked shrimp (see Simply Shrimp recipe in this chapter)
¼ cup peeled and diced mango
1 medium Roma tomato, cored, seeded, and diced
2 tablespoons peeled and diced red onion
1 tablespoon chopped fresh parsley
2 teaspoons fresh lime juice
¼ teaspoon salt
¼ teaspoon freshly ground black pepper

For Cod
2 (6-ounce) cod fillets
2 teaspoons Cajun seasoning

1. **To make Shrimp Mango Salsa:** Combine all ingredients in a medium bowl. Refrigerate covered until ready to use.

2. **To make Cod:** Preheat air fryer at 350°F for 3 minutes.

3. Season cod with Cajun seasoning. Place fish in air fryer basket lightly greased with olive oil.

4. Cook cod 10 minutes until opaque and flakes easily with a fork.

5. Transfer cod to two medium plates and serve warm topped with Shrimp Mango Salsa.

PER SERVING

CALORIES: 191		FAT: 3g	
PROTEIN: 30g		SODIUM: 467mg	
FIBER: 1g		CARBOHYDRATES: 9g	
NET CARBOHYDRATES: 8g		SUGAR: 5g	

ALTERING THIS RECIPE
The cod can be subbed out for any flaky whitefish, such as halibut, bass, tilapia, and even branzino. If you want a little more kick, add a pepper such as a jalapeño, diced, to your salsa. And, if you like cilantro, switch out the parsley for some of this fresh herb!

Lemon Garlic Sea Bass

Sea bass is a little meatier than most whitefish like cod and halibut. In addition, its buttery nature has a melt-in-your mouth texture. Simply seasoned with lemon juice, a little garlic, and some fresh parsley, this low-carb fish dish is one for the books.

- **Hands-On Time:** 5 minutes
- **Cook Time:** 7 minutes

Serves 2

1 tablespoon butter, melted

2 cloves garlic, peeled and minced

1 tablespoon fresh lemon juice

¼ teaspoon salt

2 (6-ounce, 1"-thick) sea bass fillets

2 teaspoons chopped fresh parsley

1 Preheat air fryer at 375°F for 3 minutes.

2 In a small bowl, combine butter, garlic, lemon juice, and salt. Rub mixture over tops of fillets.

3 Place sea bass in ungreased air fryer basket. Cook 7 minutes.

4 Transfer bass to two medium plates and let rest 5 minutes, then garnish with chopped parsley. Serve warm.

PER SERVING

CALORIES: 222	FAT: 9g
PROTEIN: 32g	SODIUM: 408mg
FIBER: 0g	CARBOHYDRATES: 2g
NET CARBOHYDRATES: 1g	SUGAR: 0g

8

Vegetarian Dishes

When eating a low-carb diet, coupled with being a vegetarian, your meal options can feel that much slimmer—not to mention trying to ensure the foods you *do* eat are nutritious. Fortunately, the air fryer is here to help, providing countless choices for low-carb vegetarian recipes that still manage to save you time in the kitchen. Whether you are a full-time vegetarian or just interested in Meatless Mondays, the air fryer has got you covered.

And the low-carb vegetarian dishes in this chapter will help you hit the spot. With recipes like Mexican Topped Avocados, Vegetable-Stuffed Mushrooms, and Creamy Pesto Spaghetti Squash, you're sure to find new favorites!

Mexican Topped Avocados

If you'd like to bump up the protein factor, add some beans on top of the avocado before distributing the cheese. Some beans are higher in carbs, but they are counterbalanced by the fiber and are accepted on low-carb diets in small amounts. Try a spoonful of lentils, black beans, or pinto beans.

- **Hands-On Time:** 10 minutes
- **Cook Time:** 4 minutes

Serves 2

1 cup seeded and diced tomatoes

1 tablespoon fresh lime juice

1 teaspoon lime zest

2 tablespoons chopped fresh cilantro

1 small jalapeño, seeded and minced

2 cloves garlic, peeled and minced

1 tablespoon peeled and diced red onion

½ teaspoon salt

2 large avocados, halved and pitted

4 tablespoons vegan Cheddar shreds

1 Combine tomatoes, lime juice, lime zest, cilantro, jalapeño, garlic, onion, and salt in a medium bowl. Cover and refrigerate until ready to use.

2 Preheat air fryer at 350°F for 3 minutes.

3 Place avocado halves, cut sides up, in ungreased air fryer. Distribute cheese shreds to top of avocado halves. Cook 4 minutes.

4 Transfer avocados to a large serving plate, garnish with tomato mixture, and serve.

PER SERVING

CALORIES: 172	FAT: 14g
PROTEIN: 2g	SODIUM: 349mg
FIBER: 6g	CARBOHYDRATES: 12g
NET CARBOHYDRATES: 6g	SUGAR: 2g

Taco Tuesday Fried Avocado Lettuce Wraps

Who needs carb-filled tortillas when all of the flavor is in the filling? Top these wraps with a dollop of sour cream, or add in a dash of hot sauce if you like things spicy.

- **Hands-On Time:** 15 minutes
- **Cook Time:** 10 minutes

Serves 4

For Spicy Mayonnaise
½ cup vegan mayonnaise
2 teaspoons gochujang
1 teaspoon fresh lime juice
⅛ teaspoon salt

For Salsa
2 medium Roma tomatoes, cored, seeded, and diced
¼ cup peeled and finely diced red onion
2 cloves garlic, peeled and minced
1 tablespoon fresh lime juice
1 teaspoon fresh lime zest
¼ cup chopped fresh cilantro
1 teaspoon salt

For Avocado Fries
Egg substitute equaling 1 large egg
2 tablespoons unsweetened almond milk
1 cup almond flour
¼ cup ground flaxseed
1 large avocado, peeled, halved, pitted, and cut into 12 "fries"

For Lettuce Wraps
6 large leaves iceberg lettuce
1 cup coleslaw mix (shredded cabbage and carrot)

1 **To make Spicy Mayonnaise:** In a small bowl, combine all ingredients and refrigerate covered until ready to use.

2 **To make Salsa:** In a medium bowl, combine all ingredients and refrigerate covered until ready to use.

3 **To make Avocado Fries:** Preheat air fryer at 375°F for 3 minutes.

4 Whisk together egg substitute and almond milk in a small bowl. Combine almond flour and flaxseed in a separate shallow dish.

5 Dip avocado fries in egg substitute mixture. Dredge in almond flour mixture to coat.

6 Place half of avocado fries in ungreased air fryer basket. Cook 5 minutes, then transfer to a large serving plate. Repeat cooking with remaining avocado fries.

7 **To make Lettuce Wraps:** Add two avocado fries to each lettuce wrap. Top with coleslaw mix, spicy mayonnaise, and salsa. Serve immediately.

PER SERVING

CALORIES: 422		FAT: 37g	
PROTEIN: 11g		SODIUM: 935mg	
FIBER: 11g		CARBOHYDRATES: 23g	
NET CARBOHYDRATES: 12g		SUGAR: 6g	

Jackfruit "Fish" Fritters

Jackfruit is neutral enough to take on the flavors that you add to it, while the nori and Cajun seasonings trick the taste buds into reminding you of fish flavors.

- **Hands-On Time: 10 minutes**
- **Cook Time: 20 minutes**

Serves 4

1 (20-ounce) can jackfruit, drained and chopped

1 flax egg

1 tablespoon Dijon mustard

1 tablespoon vegan mayonnaise

1 tablespoon prepared horseradish

2 tablespoons peeled and grated yellow onion

2 tablespoons chopped fresh parsley

2 tablespoons chopped nori

2 tablespoons almond flour

1 tablespoon Cajun seasoning

¼ teaspoon garlic powder

¼ teaspoon salt

2 lemon wedges

1 Combine all ingredients except lemon wedges in a medium bowl. Refrigerate covered 15 minutes.

2 Preheat air fryer at 350°F for 3 minutes. Cut a piece of parchment paper to fit bottom of air fryer basket.

3 Form chilled mixture into twelve balls, approximately 2 tablespoons each. Place six balls in ungreased air fryer basket. Cook 10 minutes.

4 Transfer to a large plate and repeat cooking with remaining balls. Serve warm garnished with lemon wedges.

PER SERVING

CALORIES: 104	FAT: 5g
PROTEIN: 1g	SODIUM: 413mg
FIBER: 6g	CARBOHYDRATES: 11g
NET CARBOHYDRATES: 5g	SUGAR: 4g

WHAT IS A FLAX EGG?

There are many vegan and vegetarian egg substitutions on the market, but one that is easy to make in your kitchen is 2 tablespoons ground flaxseed combined with 6 tablespoons water. Let it set about 15 minutes before using in a recipe. This combination equals one large egg.

Vegetable-Stuffed Mushrooms

Whether you are entertaining guests or just entertaining your own taste buds, this recipe is filled with low-carb "meaty" flavors that will satisfy the pickiest of folks.

- **Hands-On Time:** 10 minutes
- **Cook Time:** 5 minutes

Serves 2

3 teaspoons olive oil, divided

12 whole white button mushroom caps

2 tablespoons diced white button mushroom stems

2 tablespoons small-diced yellow squash

1 teaspoon nutritional yeast

¼ teaspoon salt

2 tablespoons no-sugar-added tomato paste

1 tablespoon chopped fresh parsley

1 Brush 1 teaspoon olive oil around top ridge of mushroom caps.

2 Preheat air fryer at 350°F for 3 minutes.

3 In a medium bowl, combine mushroom stems, squash, nutritional yeast, salt, remaining olive oil, and tomato paste. Distribute and press mixture into tops of mushroom caps.

4 Place stuffed mushrooms in ungreased air fryer basket. Cook 5 minutes.

5 Transfer mushrooms to a medium plate and garnish with parsley. Serve.

PER SERVING

CALORIES: 85	FAT: 7g
PROTEIN: 2g	SODIUM: 305mg
FIBER: 1g	CARBOHYDRATES: 5g
NET CARBOHYDRATES: 4g	SUGAR: 3g

Mushroom and Onion Pizza Rounds

Serve these low-carb pizza rounds alongside a fresh mixed green salad for a tummy full of healthy ingredients. If you don't eat dairy, there are excellent vegan mozzarella shreds available that can be substituted in this recipe.

- **Hands-On Time: 10 minutes**
- **Cook Time: 15 minutes**

Serves 4

2 teaspoons plus 2 tablespoons olive oil, divided

¼ cup peeled and small-diced yellow onion

½ cup small-diced baby bella mushrooms

½ cup no-sugar-added marinara sauce

1 small eggplant, sliced into 8½" circles

1 teaspoon salt

1 cup shredded mozzarella

¼ cup chopped fresh basil

1 In a medium skillet, heat 2 teaspoons olive oil over medium heat 30 seconds. Add onion and mushrooms. Cook 4 minutes until onion is translucent. Add marinara sauce and stir. Remove from heat.

2 Preheat air fryer at 375°F for 3 minutes.

3 Rub remaining 2 tablespoons olive oil over both sides of eggplant circles. Lay out slices on a large plate and season evenly with salt. Top evenly with sauce mixture and shredded mozzarella.

4 Place half of eggplant pizzas in ungreased air fryer basket. Cook 5 minutes. Transfer back to plate. Repeat cooking with remaining pizzas.

5 Garnish pizzas with chopped basil and serve warm.

PER SERVING

CALORIES: 179	FAT: 14g
PROTEIN: 8g	SODIUM: 816mg
FIBER: 2g	CARBOHYDRATES: 6g
NET CARBOHYDRATES: 4g	SUGAR: 3g

Barbecue Jackfruit Lettuce Wraps with Coleslaw

Whether you like your barbecue sauce spicy or neutral, choose a sugar-free version to keep things low-carb. The jackfruit will take on its favor, and the cool coleslaw will meld nicely with whatever sauce you choose.

- **Hands-On Time:** 10 minutes
- **Cook Time:** 10 minutes

Serves 3

For Coleslaw
1 cup prepackaged coleslaw mix
¼ cup vegan mayonnaise
2 teaspoons granular erythritol
½ teaspoon apple cider vinegar
¼ teaspoon salt
¼ teaspoon freshly ground black pepper

For Jackfruit Wraps
1 (20-ounce) can green jackfruit in brine, drained and diced
⅔ cup sugar-free barbecue sauce, divided
6 large leaves iceberg lettuce

1 **To make Coleslaw:** In a medium bowl, combine all ingredients. Refrigerate covered until ready to use.

2 **To make Jackfruit Wraps:** Preheat air fryer at 375°F for 3 minutes.

3 Toss ⅓ cup barbecue sauce with jackfruit in a medium bowl.

4 Place jackfruit in air fryer basket lightly greased with olive oil and cook 5 minutes. Shake basket. Cook an additional 5 minutes.

5 Transfer jackfruit to a medium bowl. Add remaining sauce. Using two forks, pull apart jackfruit until it resembles pulled pork.

6 Serve jackfruit on lettuce leaves topped with coleslaw.

PER SERVING

CALORIES: 193	FAT: 10g
PROTEIN: 1g	SODIUM: 895mg
FIBER: 9g	CARBOHYDRATES: 22g
NET CARBOHYDRATES: 11g	SUGAR: 25g

WHAT IS JACKFRUIT?

Jackfruit is a highly nutritious fruit that can be found fresh or canned. Depending on the ripeness of the fruit, it can be used in sweet or savory dishes. When not ripened, it has a neutral flavor that makes it an amazing meat replacement that will take on the flavor it is paired with.

Greek Eggplant Rounds

Eggplant comes in many varieties and shapes. Although any eggplant will work with this recipe, try picking up a graffiti eggplant or Chinese eggplant, as they tend to be longer and slimmer, yielding more consistent rounds.

- **Hands-On Time:** 10 minutes
- **Cook Time:** 10 minutes

Serves 4

2 teaspoons olive oil

1 long, narrow eggplant, sliced into rounds

½ teaspoon salt

½ cup no-sugar-added marinara sauce

½ cup feta cheese crumbles

8 kalamata olives, pitted and halved

2 tablespoons chopped fresh dill

1 Preheat air fryer at 350°F for 3 minutes.

2 Rub olive oil over both sides of eggplant circles. Lay out slices on a large plate and season evenly with salt. Top evenly with marinara sauce, feta crumbles, and olives.

3 Place half of eggplant pizzas in ungreased air fryer basket. Cook 5 minutes. Transfer back to plate. Repeat cooking with remaining pizzas.

4 Garnish with chopped dill and serve warm.

PER SERVING

CALORIES: 82	FAT: 5g
PROTEIN: 2g	SODIUM: 387mg
FIBER: 2g	CARBOHYDRATES: 7g
NET CARBOHYDRATES: 5g	SUGAR: 4g

Buddha Bowls

Packed with vegetables, riced cauliflower, arugula, and pine nuts, these low-carb bowls are overflowing with flavor, texture, and nutrition. The heartiness of the ingredients will ensure that you stay full and satisfied for many hours.

- **Hands-On Time: 5 minutes**
- **Cook Time: 14 minutes**

Serves 4

1 large carrot, peeled and julienned

¼ cup apple cider vinegar

½ teaspoon ground ginger

⅛ teaspoon cayenne pepper

½ small yellow onion, peeled and sliced into half-moons

1 medium parsnip, peeled and diced

1 teaspoon avocado oil

4 ounces extra-firm tofu, drained and cut into ¼″ cubes

½ teaspoon five-spice powder

½ teaspoon chili powder

2 teaspoons fresh lime zest

1 cup fresh arugula

½ cup steamed riced cauliflower

1 small avocado, peeled, pitted, and diced

2 tablespoons pine nuts

1 Preheat air fryer at 350°F for 3 minutes.

2 In a small bowl, combine carrot, apple cider vinegar, ginger, and cayenne. Set aside.

3 In a separate small bowl, combine onion, parsnip, and avocado oil. Set aside.

4 In a medium bowl, combine tofu, five-spice powder, and chili powder.

5 Place onion mixture in air fryer basket lightly greased with olive oil. Cook 6 minutes. Add tofu mixture and toss. Cook an additional 8 minutes. Stir in lime zest.

6 Prepare Buddha Bowls by evenly distributing arugula, drained carrot juliennes, riced cauliflower, avocado, pine nuts, and tofu mixture between two medium bowls. Serve.

PER SERVING

CALORIES: 183	FAT: 13g
PROTEIN: 6g	SODIUM: 48mg
FIBER: 6g	CARBOHYDRATES: 14g
NET CARBOHYDRATES: 8g	SUGAR: 4g

Curried Tofu and Turmeric Cauli Rice

To ensure nice and crispy tofu, both drain it and use paper towels to gently press the excess moisture out before cutting the tofu into cubes.

- **Hands-On Time:** 5 minutes
- **Cook Time:** 16 minutes

Serves 4

8 ounces extra-firm tofu, pressed and cut into ¼" cubes

½ cup canned unsweetened coconut milk

2 teaspoons red curry paste

2 cloves garlic, peeled and minced

1 tablespoon avocado oil

1 tablespoon coconut oil

1 small head cauliflower, pulsed into rice

1 tablespoon turmeric powder

½ teaspoon salt

½ teaspoon freshly ground white pepper

4 lime wedges

¼ cup chopped fresh cilantro

1 In a medium bowl, combine tofu, coconut milk, red curry paste, garlic, and avocado oil. Refrigerate covered 30 minutes.

2 Preheat air fryer at 350°F for 3 minutes.

3 Place tofu and marinade in an ungreased cake barrel. Place in air fryer basket and cook 5 minutes. Stir, then cook an additional 5 minutes.

4 While tofu is cooking, heat coconut oil in a medium skillet over medium-high heat for 30 seconds. Add riced cauliflower, turmeric powder, salt, and pepper. Stir-fry 6 minutes until cauliflower is tender to your preference.

5 Add cauliflower to four medium bowls. Top with tofu mixture and sauce. Garnish with lime wedges and cilantro. Serve warm.

PER SERVING

CALORIES: 177	FAT: 12g
PROTEIN: 9g	SODIUM: 532mg
FIBER: 4g	CARBOHYDRATES: 12g
NET CARBOHYDRATES: 7g	SUGAR: 3g

Korean Ground "Beef" and Kimchi Bowls

Packed with beautiful flavors, this dish would be great over a bed of low-carb cauliflower rice or zoodles. Add a little coconut aminos to either of these bases when heating up.

- **Hands-On Time: 10 minutes**
- **Cook Time: 8 minutes**

Serves 4

2 cups beefless grounds

1 medium carrot, peeled and julienned

6 scallions, sliced, 2 tablespoons greens reserved for garnish

1 medium zucchini, diced

2 tablespoons coconut aminos

2 teaspoons sesame oil

1 teaspoon apple cider vinegar

2 teaspoons granular erythritol

1 tablespoon gochujang

¼ teaspoon salt

½ cup kimchi

2 teaspoons roasted sesame seeds

1. Preheat air fryer at 350°F for 3 minutes.

2. In a large bowl, combine beefless grounds, carrot, scallions, zucchini, coconut aminos, sesame oil, apple cider vinegar, erythritol, gochujang, and salt.

3. Place mixture in an ungreased cake barrel. Place barrel in air fryer basket and cook 6 minutes. Stir in kimchi. Cook an additional 2 minutes.

4. Transfer to two medium bowls and garnish with reserved scallion greens and roasted sesame seeds. Serve.

PER SERVING

CALORIES: 157	FAT: 7g
PROTEIN: 15g	SODIUM: 762mg
FIBER: 4g	CARBOHYDRATES: 14g
NET CARBOHYDRATES: 8g	SUGAR: 6g

WHERE DO I FIND ROASTED SESAME SEEDS?

You can purchase preroasted sesame seeds in most grocery stores. However, if you can find only unroasted ones, it's easy to roast them yourself. Place your unroasted seeds in a small ungreased skillet over low heat. Using a spatula, push the seeds around in the skillet until they are golden brown, about 3 minutes.

Caprese Hasselback Tomatoes

With this recipe, you don't want the cheese to be completely melted. The air fryer simply softens up the mozzarella while heating the tomatoes just enough to bring out their natural sugars. And don't forget to use fresh basil leaves: They are everything in a caprese dish!

- **Hands-On Time:** 10 minutes
- **Cook Time:** 3 minutes

Serves 4

4 medium Roma tomatoes, bottoms removed to create flat surfaces

16 fresh basil leaves

1 (8-ounce) ball fresh mozzarella, sliced and then cut into 16 pieces

½ teaspoon salt

½ teaspoon freshly ground black pepper

1 tablespoon olive oil

2 teaspoons balsamic vinegar

1 Preheat air fryer at 325°F for 3 minutes.

2 Make four even slices on each tomato, three-quarters of the way down. Stuff one basil leaf and a piece of mozzarella into each slice. Season with salt and pepper.

3 Place stuffed tomatoes in ungreased air fryer basket. Cook 3 minutes. Transfer to a large serving plate.

4 Drizzle tomatoes with olive oil and balsamic vinegar and serve.

PER SERVING

CALORIES: 201	FAT: 15g
PROTEIN: 12g	SODIUM: 522mg
FIBER: 2g	CARBOHYDRATES: 5g
NET CARBOHYDRATES: 4g	SUGAR: 4g

Stuffed Bell Peppers

Bell peppers are just one of those vegetables that take on a different flavor once cooked. Tender and flavorful, these peppers are stuffed with a blend of tomatoes, onions, squash, and seasonings, with the addition of mushrooms to lend a "meaty" touch.

- **Hands-On Time:** 15 minutes
- **Cook Time:** 22 minutes

Serves 4

2 medium bell peppers, color of choice

4 teaspoons olive oil, divided

½ medium yellow onion, peeled and finely diced

¾ cup finely diced summer squash

¾ cup chopped baby bella (cremini) mushrooms

½ cup canned fire-roasted diced tomatoes, including juice

¼ cup tomato sauce

2 teaspoons Italian seasoning

¼ teaspoon smoked paprika

½ teaspoon salt

¼ teaspoon freshly ground black pepper

1 Cut bell peppers in half from top to bottom and seed them. Brush inside and tops of bell peppers with 2 teaspoons olive oil. Set aside.

2 In a medium skillet, heat remaining oil over medium-high heat 30 seconds. Add onion, squash, and mushrooms. Stir-fry 5 minutes until onions are tender.

3 In a medium bowl, combine tomatoes, tomato sauce, Italian seasoning, smoked paprika, salt, and pepper.

4 Preheat air fryer at 350°F for 3 minutes.

5 Evenly distribute mixture among the bell pepper halves.

6 Place two halves in the air fryer basket. Cook 8 minutes.

7 Transfer to a serving plate. Continue with remaining halves. Serve warm.

PER SERVING

CALORIES: 81	FAT: 5g
PROTEIN: 2g	SODIUM: 409mg
FIBER: 3g	CARBOHYDRATES: 8g
NET CARBOHYDRATES: 6g	SUGAR: 5g

Creamy Pesto Spaghetti Squash

Once cooked, the long strands of squash that resemble spaghetti noodles will be easily pulled out—and even spun around on your fork in true Italian fashion!

- **Hands-On Time: 5 minutes**
- **Cook Time: 25 minutes**

Serves 4

2 teaspoons olive oil

1 (1½-pound) spaghetti squash, halved and seeded

½ teaspoon salt, divided

½ cup pesto

½ cup ricotta cheese

2 tablespoons chopped fresh basil leaves

HOMEMADE PESTO

Although there are several great varieties of pesto on the market, you can also make your own. For a traditional pesto, pulse the following ingredients together: 1 cup fresh basil leaves, ¼ cup fresh parsley, ⅛ teaspoon salt, 4 cloves peeled garlic, ¼ cup raw pine nuts, ½ cup Parmesan cheese (substitute ¼ cup nutritional yeast if you don't eat cheese), and 3 tablespoons olive oil.

1 Preheat air fryer at 375°F for 3 minutes.

2 Rub olive oil over both halves of spaghetti squash. Season with half of salt. Place both halves, flat sides down, in ungreased air fryer basket. Cook 25 minutes.

3 Transfer squash to a cutting board and let cool for 5 minutes until easy to handle. Once cooled, use a fork to gently pull the strands out of squash and place into a medium bowl.

4 Toss squash noodles with pesto, ricotta cheese, and remaining salt. Garnish with basil leaves. Serve warm.

PER SERVING

CALORIES: 243	**FAT:** 20g
PROTEIN: 6g	**SODIUM:** 647mg
FIBER: 3g	**CARBOHYDRATES:** 12g
NET CARBOHYDRATES: 10g	**SUGAR:** 5g

Baba Ghanoush

This bold and flavorful Middle Eastern eggplant dish is not only tasty but also so healthy—and so surprisingly low-carb! The air fryer helps lend that smoky element to this classic dip.

- **Hands-On Time:** 5 minutes
- **Cook Time:** 27 minutes

Serves 4

3 teaspoons olive oil, divided

1 medium eggplant, halved lengthwise

2 teaspoons pine nuts

¼ cup tahini

1 tablespoon lemon juice

2 cloves garlic, peeled and minced

⅛ teaspoon ground cumin

¼ teaspoon salt

⅛ teaspoon freshly ground black pepper

1 tablespoon chopped fresh parsley

1 Preheat air fryer at 375°F for 3 minutes.

2 Rub 2 teaspoons olive oil over both eggplant halves. Pierce eggplant flesh a few times with a fork. Place eggplant, flat sides down, in ungreased air fryer basket. Cook 25 minutes.

3 Transfer eggplant to a cutting board and let cool for 3 minutes until easy to handle.

4 While eggplant cools, add pine nuts to ungreased air fryer basket. Cook 2 minutes, shaking every 30 seconds to ensure they don't burn. Set aside in a small bowl.

5 Scoop out eggplant flesh and add to a food processor. Pulse together with tahini, lemon juice, garlic, cumin, salt, and pepper. Transfer to a medium serving bowl. Garnish with roasted pine nuts, parsley, and remaining olive oil. Serve.

WHAT ARE CRUDITÉS?

Crudités is just a fancy word for chopped vegetables. So, cut up some carrots, celery, cauliflower, cucumbers, radishes, and bell peppers—or whatever other vegetables your taste buds desire—and you have yourself a freshly-chopped crudités treat which is a great companion to this recipe. You are limited only by the produce section!

PER SERVING

CALORIES: 166	**FAT:** 13g
PROTEIN: 4g	**SODIUM:** 154mg
FIBER: 5g	**CARBOHYDRATES:** 12g
NET CARBOHYDRATES: 8g	**SUGAR:** 4g

Spaghetti Squash with Avocado Sauce

The avocado sauce is so creamy, and the nutritional yeast gives a hint of cheese flavor. Cooked mushrooms would also be a great addition to this recipe.

- **Hands-On Time: 5 minutes**
- **Cook Time: 25 minutes**

Serves 4

2 teaspoons olive oil

1 (1½-pound) spaghetti squash, halved and seeded

1 teaspoon salt, divided

1 medium ripe avocado, peeled and pitted

⅓ cup vegetable broth

2 teaspoons nutritional yeast

2 medium Campari tomatoes, diced

1 Preheat air fryer at 375°F for 3 minutes.

2 Rub olive oil over both halves of spaghetti squash. Season with ¾ teaspoon salt. Place flat sides down in ungreased air fryer basket. Cook 25 minutes.

3 While squash is cooking, blend together avocado, vegetable broth, nutritional yeast, and remaining ¼ teaspoon salt. Set aside.

4 Transfer cooked squash to a cutting board and let cool for 4 minutes until easy to handle. Once cooled, use a fork to gently pull strands out of squash into a medium serving bowl. Toss with avocado sauce. Garnish with fresh tomato.

PER SERVING

CALORIES: 152	**FAT:** 10g
PROTEIN: 3g	**SODIUM:** 672mg
FIBER: 6g	**CARBOHYDRATES:** 17g
NET CARBOHYDRATES: 10g	**SUGAR:** 5g

Chili-Roasted Vegetable Bowls

These hearty bowls of vegetables are enhanced with a little kick of chili flavor. Don't be afraid to experiment with your favorite vegetables!

- **Hands-On Time:** 15 minutes
- **Cook Time:** 15 minutes

Serves 4

1 cup quartered Brussels sprouts

1 cup broccoli florets

½ small yellow onion, peeled and sliced into half-moons

1 medium red bell pepper, seeded and sliced

1 medium yellow bell pepper, seeded and sliced

1 tablespoon olive oil

½ teaspoon chili powder

¼ teaspoon ground cumin

¼ teaspoon ground coriander

1 Preheat air fryer at 350°F for 3 minutes.

2 In a large bowl, combine Brussels sprouts, broccoli, onion, and bell peppers. Toss with olive oil, chili powder, cumin, and coriander.

3 Add vegetable mixture to ungreased air fryer basket. Cook 15 minutes, tossing every 5 minutes.

4 Transfer to four medium bowls and serve warm.

PER SERVING

CALORIES: 70	FAT: 4g
PROTEIN: 2g	SODIUM: 23mg
FIBER: 3g	CARBOHYDRATES: 8g
NET CARBOHYDRATES: 5g	SUGAR: 4g

"Fauxtato" Shepherdless Pie

"Fauxtato" Shepherdless Pie delivers all the punch of the classic version, without the meat and carbs. The rich filling is topped with a creamy and cheesy mashed "fauxtato" topping. For a decorative effect, pipe dollops of the mashed "fauxtatoes" on top before cooking.

- **Hands-On Time:** 15 minutes
- **Cook Time:** 23 minutes

Serves 6

For Topping
½ small head cauliflower, cut into florets
1 small parsnip, peeled and diced
1 tablespoon avocado oil
¼ cup nondairy Cheddar shreds
2 tablespoons almond milk
½ teaspoon salt
½ teaspoon freshly ground black pepper

For Filling
2 teaspoons avocado oil
1 cup beefless grounds
½ small yellow onion, peeled and diced
2 cloves garlic, peeled and minced
1 medium carrot, peeled and diced
¼ cup seeded and diced green bell pepper
1 small stalk celery, diced
⅔ cup no-sugar-added tomato sauce
1 teaspoon chopped fresh rosemary
1 teaspoon fresh thyme leaves
½ teaspoon salt
½ teaspoon freshly ground black pepper

1 **To make Topping:** Add cauliflower and parsnip to a medium pot of salted boiling water over high heat for 7 minutes until fork-tender.

2 Drain cauliflower and parsnip and transfer to a medium bowl. Add avocado oil, Cheddar shreds, almond milk, salt, and pepper. Mash until smooth.

3 **To make Filling:** While cauliflower and parsnips are cooking, add avocado oil to a large skillet over medium-high heat. Toss in beefless grounds, onion, garlic, carrot, bell pepper, and celery and cook 4 minutes until vegetables are tender. Add tomato sauce, rosemary, thyme, salt, and black pepper. Set aside.

4 **To assemble:** Preheat air fryer at 350°F for 3 minutes.

5 Spoon filling into a round cake barrel lightly greased with olive oil. Top with topping. Using the tines of a fork, run shallow lines in the top of the cauliflower for a decorative touch. Cook 12 minutes.

6 Remove barrel from air fryer and let rest 10 minutes in barrel, then serve warm.

PER SERVING

CALORIES: 136	FAT: 7g
PROTEIN: 6g	SODIUM: 655mg
FIBER: 3g	CARBOHYDRATES: 12g
NET CARBOHYDRATES: 9g	SUGAR: 4g

Broccoli Casserole

People who don't really care for broccoli will find themselves scooping up a second helping of this creamy casserole.

- **Hands-On Time: 15 minutes**
- **Cook Time: 14 minutes**

Serves 4

4 cups steamed broccoli florets (about 1 large head), chopped

¼ cup peeled diced yellow onion

½ cup diced white mushrooms

1 large egg

2 tablespoons sour cream

¼ cup mayonnaise

1 teaspoon salt

½ teaspoon freshly ground black pepper

1 cup coarsely crushed Cheddar cheese crisps

1 In a large bowl, combine broccoli, onion, mushrooms, egg, sour cream, mayonnaise, salt, and pepper. Spoon mixture into a round cake barrel.

2 Preheat air fryer at 350°F for 3 minutes.

3 Cook casserole 14 minutes.

4 Remove barrel from air fryer and let rest 10 minutes. Evenly distribute crushed Cheddar Cheese crisps over the top of casserole and serve warm.

PER SERVING

CALORIES: 251	FAT: 21g
PROTEIN: 10g	SODIUM: 896mg
FIBER: 3g	CARBOHYDRATES: 8g
NET CARBOHYDRATES: 6g	SUGAR: 2g

Vegan Dogs and Sauerkraut

Your air fryer is the perfect appliance for cooking hot dogs. When you want that grill flavor, but don't have the time, just break out the air fryer and in no time you will be on your very own personal picnic.

- **Hands-On Time: 5 minutes**
- **Cook Time: 5 minutes**

Serves 2

4 vegan hot dogs
2 cups sauerkraut
2 tablespoons German mustard

HOMEMADE SAUERKRAUT

Fermenting vegetables can seem very scary to those who have never tried it. Let sauerkraut be your gateway into a fun new world. Sauerkraut consists of just two ingredients: cabbage and salt. You'll find all the details online for fermenting your own in a few easy steps.

1 Preheat air fryer to 400°F for 3 minutes.

2 Add hot dogs to ungreased air fryer basket. Cook 5 minutes.

3 Transfer hot dogs to a large plate and serve warm with sauerkraut and mustard.

PER SERVING

CALORIES: 137	FAT: 2g
PROTEIN: 16g	SODIUM: 1,965mg
FIBER: 6g	CARBOHYDRATES: 16g
NET CARBOHYDRATES: 10g	SUGAR: 6g

9

Desserts

Enjoying sweet treats can seem almost impossible when eating a low-carb diet. All of those cakes, pies, cobblers, and cookies are usually filled with one pesky, carb-filled ingredient: sugar. But that doesn't mean you have to ignore your sweet tooth. In fact, there are dozens of sugar substitutes available that allow you to create low-carb desserts that are just as yummy (if not more so) as the original recipes. And the air fryer is here to make them even easier to bake!

With recipes ranging from Ultimate Chocolate Brownies and Blueberry Crumble Jars to Nutty Pumpkin Mug Cake, the mouthwatering delights in this chapter are guaranteed to hit the spot—no matter what you find yourself craving.

Ultimate Chocolate Brownies

What is better than chocolate? Double chocolate! And the crunch of the pecans is a natural addition to these brownies, although crushed almonds or walnuts work just as well! For presentation, dust a little powdered erythritol on the finished bake.

- **Hands-On Time:** 10 minutes
- **Cook Time:** 11 minutes

Yields 9 brownies

⅓ cup almond flour

¼ cup unsweetened cocoa

½ cup powdered erythritol

½ teaspoon baking soda

3 tablespoons unsalted butter, melted

1 tablespoon sour cream

1 large egg

⅛ teaspoon salt

¼ cup sugar-free semisweet chocolate chips

¼ cup chopped pecans

1   Preheat air fryer at 350°F for 3 minutes.

2   In a medium bowl, combine flour, cocoa, erythritol, baking soda, butter, and sour cream. Stir in egg and salt. Add chocolate chips and chopped pecans, stirring until mixture is thick and sticky.

3   Press mixture into a square cake barrel greased with cooking spray. Cover pan with aluminum foil and place in air fryer basket. Cook 9 minutes. Remove foil and cook an additional 2 minutes.

4   Remove pan from air fryer and let cool 30 minutes. Once cooled, slice into nine sections and serve.

PER SERVING (1 BROWNIE)

CALORIES: 126	FAT: 11g
PROTEIN: 3g	SODIUM: 63mg
FIBER: 2g	CARBOHYDRATES: 18g
NET CARBOHYDRATES: 2g	SUGAR: 0g

Giant Chocolate Chip Cookie

This chocolate chip cookie is thinner than a cake but thicker than a cookie—with all the flavor you love. Top with sugar-free whipped cream for an extra special treat.

- **Hands-On Time:** 10 minutes
- **Cook Time:** 8 minutes

Yields 9 cookies

⅓ cup almond flour

2 tablespoons powdered erythritol

1 large egg

½ teaspoon vanilla extract

3 tablespoons butter, melted

⅛ teaspoon salt

2 tablespoons sugar-free dark chocolate chips

1 Preheat air fryer at 350°F for 3 minutes.

2 In a medium bowl, combine all ingredients except chocolate chips. Fold in chocolate chips.

3 Spoon mixture into a pizza pan greased with cooking spray. Place pan in air fryer basket and cook 8 minutes.

4 Slice and serve warm.

PER SERVING (1 COOKIE)

CALORIES: 82	FAT: 7g
PROTEIN: 2g	SODIUM: 42mg
FIBER: 1g	CARBOHYDRATES: 6g
NET CARBOHYDRATES: 1g	SUGAR: 0g

Giant Peanut Butter Cookie

The powdered peanut butter contains less natural fat because the peanuts have been pressed down and then ground into a fine powder. It lends a peanut butter flavor to cookies, smoothies, and even low-carb pancakes!

- **Hands-On Time:** 10 minutes
- **Cook Time:** 8 minutes

Yields 9 cookies

⅓ cup almond flour

¼ cup powdered erythritol

1 large egg

½ teaspoon vanilla extract

4 tablespoons butter, melted

⅛ teaspoon salt

4 tablespoons powdered peanut butter

1 Preheat air fryer at 350°F for 3 minutes.

2 In a medium bowl, combine all ingredients.

3 Spoon mixture into a pizza pan greased with cooking spray. Place pan in air fryer basket and cook 8 minutes.

4 Slice and serve warm.

PER SERVING (1 COOKIE)

CALORIES: 89	FAT: 8g
PROTEIN: 3g	SODIUM: 63mg
FIBER: 1g	CARBOHYDRATES: 7g
NET CARBOHYDRATES: 1g	SUGAR: 0g

Strawberry Cake with Orange Glaze

This fresh cake is filled with chopped strawberries, lending a moistness to every bite. The orange in the glaze pairs nicely with the berry flavor. Pour a cup of tea, pull up a chair, and cut yourself a slice!

- **Hands-On Time:** 10 minutes
- **Cook Time:** 10 minutes

Serves 4

For Cake
½ cup finely ground almond flour
¼ cup powdered erythritol
½ teaspoon baking powder
⅛ teaspoon salt
2 tablespoons butter, melted
1 large egg
2 teaspoons orange zest
½ teaspoon unflavored gelatin
½ teaspoon vanilla extract
½ teaspoon ground cinnamon
¼ cup hulled and finely chopped strawberries

For Glaze
1 tablespoon butter, melted
¼ teaspoon orange zest
1 tablespoon orange juice
¼ cup powdered erythritol

1 **To make Cake:** Preheat air fryer at 300°F for 3 minutes.

2 In a large bowl, combine flour, erythritol, baking powder, and salt. Set aside.

3 In a small bowl, combine butter, egg, orange zest, gelatin, vanilla, cinnamon, strawberries. Add to flour mixture and stir until combined.

4 Spoon mixture into an ungreased pizza pan. Place pan in air fryer basket and cook 10 minutes. Remove pan from basket and let set about 30 minutes until cooled.

5 **To make Glaze:** Combine butter, orange zest, orange juice, and erythritol in a small bowl. Add a little water if glaze is too thick and a little extra erythritol if glaze is too thin. Pour over cooled cake.

6 Slice cake and serve.

PER SERVING

CALORIES: 183	**FAT:** 17g
PROTEIN: 5g	**SODIUM:** 143mg
FIBER: 2g	**CARBOHYDRATES:** 29g
NET CARBOHYDRATES: 3g	**SUGAR:** 2g

Almond Ricotta Lime Cake

This bright and tasty low-carb delicacy is an ideal dessert for any night of the week, or even a nice start to your day alongside a warm cup of tea or coffee.

- **Hands-On Time:** 5 minutes
- **Cook Time:** 15 minutes

Serves 2

For Cake
1 cup finely ground almond flour
⅓ cup powdered erythritol
1 teaspoon baking powder
½ teaspoon cream of tartar
⅛ teaspoon salt
2 large eggs
½ cup ricotta cheese
1 tablespoon butter, melted
½ teaspoon vanilla extract
½ teaspoon lime zest
1 tablespoon lime juice

For Topping
1 tablespoon butter, melted
¼ teaspoon lime zest
2 teaspoons lime juice
¼ cup plus 1 tablespoon powdered erythritol, divided
2 tablespoons sliced almonds

1 **To make Cake:** Preheat air fryer at 300°F for 3 minutes.

2 In a large bowl, combine flour, erythritol, baking powder, cream of tartar, and salt. Stir in eggs, ricotta cheese, butter, vanilla, lime zest, and lime juice until combined.

3 Spoon mixture into a 7" springform pan greased with cooking spray. Place pan in air fryer basket and cook 15 minutes.

4 Remove pan from basket and let cool 10 minutes, then remove sides of springform pan.

5 **To make Topping:** Combine butter, lime zest, lime juice, and ¼ cup erythritol in a small bowl. Consistency should be a little thicker than a glaze. Spread over top of cooled cake.

6 Garnish with almonds and remaining erythritol. Slice and serve.

PER SERVING

CALORIES: 644	FAT: 55g
PROTEIN: 27g	SODIUM: 472mg
FIBER: 7g	CARBOHYDRATES: 80g
NET CARBOHYDRATES: 11g	SUGAR: 3g

Double Chocolate Cake

When chocolate is screaming your name but you don't want the sugar, this low-carb cake for two will hit your craving in the right place. It's also great with a scoop of sugar-free ice cream!

- **Hands-On Time: 5 minutes**
- **Cook Time: 15 minutes**

Serves 2

For Cake
⅔ cup finely ground almond flour
¼ cup cocoa
⅓ cup powdered erythritol
1 teaspoon baking powder
⅛ teaspoon salt
⅛ teaspoon ground cinnamon
⅛ teaspoon chili powder
4 tablespoons butter, melted
2 large eggs
1 teaspoon vanilla extract

For Chocolate Ganache
¼ cup sugar-free chocolate chips
2 tablespoons heavy cream
1 tablespoon powdered erythritol

1 **To make Cake:** Preheat air fryer at 350° for 3 minutes.

2 In a large bowl, combine flour, cocoa, erythritol, baking powder, salt, cinnamon, and chili powder. Set aside.

3 In a small bowl, combine butter, eggs, and vanilla. Add to flour mixture and stir until smooth.

4 Spoon mixture into a cake barrel lightly greased with olive oil. Place barrel in air fryer basket and cook 11 minutes.

5 Remove barrel from basket and let set until cool, about 10 minutes.

6 **To make Chocolate Ganache:** In a double boiler, add all ingredients and place over medium heat. Continuously whisk mixture until smooth, about 4 minutes.

7 Pour ganache over cooled cake and let set for 30 minutes. Slice and serve.

PER SERVING

CALORIES: 712	FAT: 62g
PROTEIN: 19g	SODIUM: 426mg
FIBER: 10g	CARBOHYDRATES: 72g
NET CARBOHYDRATES: 10g	SUGAR: 2g

Blueberry Crumble Jars

Serve this portable low-carb delight with some fresh whipped cream or sugar-free vanilla ice cream.

- **Hands-On Time:** 10 minutes
- **Cook Time:** 24 minutes

Serves 6

For Blueberry Filling
3 cups fresh blueberries
2 tablespoons almond flour
1 tablespoon pulp-free orange juice
2 teaspoons orange zest
¼ cup granular erythritol
1 tablespoon butter, melted
⅛ teaspoon salt
6 (4-ounce) oven-safe glass jelly jars

For Crumble Topping
2 tablespoons almond flour
2 tablespoons granular erythritol
4 tablespoons pecan pieces
2 tablespoons slivered almonds
2 tablespoons unsweetened coconut flakes
2 tablespoons unsalted sunflower seeds
3 tablespoons butter, melted

1 **To make Blueberry Filling:** Preheat air fryer at 350°F for 3 minutes.

2 Combine all ingredients in a large bowl. Distribute evenly into jelly jars.

3 Place three jars in air fryer basket. Cook 7 minutes. Repeat cooking with remaining jars. When jars are removed from air fryer, use the back of a spoon to gently press down on the blueberry filling. Set aside.

4 **To make Crumble Topping:** Combine all ingredients in a medium bowl. Distribute mixture over cooked filling in jars.

5 Place three jars back in air fryer and cook an additional 5 minutes. Repeat cooking with remaining jars.

6 Let jars cool 10 minutes before eating or covering. Refrigerate until ready to serve, up to four days.

PER SERVING

CALORIES: 204	FAT: 16g
PROTEIN: 3g	SODIUM: 57mg
FIBER: 3g	CARBOHYDRATES: 27g
NET CARBOHYDRATES: 11g	SUGAR: 9g

USING JELLY JARS

Jelly jars are traditionally used for canning but serve other purposes as well. By making desserts in these jars, it not only preportions your recipes, but it also makes them portable for easy grab-and-go lunch additions.

Ginger Strawberry Crumble Jars

The freshly grated ginger in this dessert adds a zippy counterpart to the fresh, sweet strawberries. Already portioned out, the jars are easy to store and bring along for a picnic, hike, or your lunchbox!

- **Hands-On Time:** 10 minutes
- **Cook Time:** 24 minutes

Serves 6

For Filling
3 cups hulled and small-diced fresh strawberries
2 tablespoons almond flour
2 teaspoons peeled and grated fresh ginger
1 tablespoon lime juice
2 teaspoons lime zest
¼ cup granular erythritol
1 tablespoon butter, melted
⅛ teaspoon salt
6 (4-ounce) glass jelly jars

For Crumble Topping
2 tablespoons almond flour
2 tablespoons granular erythritol
1 teaspoon peeled and grated fresh ginger
4 tablespoons pecan pieces
2 tablespoons slivered almonds
2 tablespoons unsweetened coconut flakes
2 tablespoons unsalted sunflower seeds
3 tablespoons butter, melted

1 **To make Filling:** Preheat air fryer at 350°F for 3 minutes.

2 Combine strawberries, almond flour, ginger, lime juice, lime zest, erythritol, butter, and salt in a medium bowl. Distribute into jelly jars.

3 Place three jars in air fryer basket. Cook 7 minutes. Repeat cooking with remaining jars. When jars are removed from air fryer, use the back of a spoon and gently press down on the strawberry filling. Set aside.

4 **To make Crumble Topping:** Combine all ingredients in a medium bowl. Distribute mixture on top of cooked filling.

5 Add three jars back to air fryer and cook an additional 5 minutes. Repeat cooking with remaining jars.

6 Let jars cool 10 minutes before eating or covering. Refrigerate until ready to serve, up to four days.

PER SERVING

CALORIES: 192	FAT: 17g
PROTEIN: 3g	SODIUM: 53mg
FIBER: 4g	CARBOHYDRATES: 22g
NET CARBOHYDRATES: 6g	SUGAR: 5g

Key Lime Cheesecake

Key limes tend to be seasonal in the United States, so if you can't find any, just substitute for half lime juice and half lemon juice. In fact, most any citrus fruit will yield a tasty treat: Try blood oranges for an exotic twist.

- **Hands-On Time: 10 minutes**
- **Cook Time: 19 minutes**

Serves 6

1 cup ground walnuts (walnut meal)

3 tablespoons butter, melted

3 tablespoons granular erythritol

12 ounces cream cheese, room temperature

2 tablespoons sour cream

2 large eggs

¼ cup powdered erythritol

1 tablespoon key lime zest

1 tablespoon fresh key lime juice

1 teaspoon vanilla extract

⅛ teaspoon salt

1 Preheat air fryer at 400°F for 3 minutes.

2 Combine ground walnuts, butter, and granular erythritol in a medium bowl. Press mixture into an ungreased 7" springform pan.

3 Place pan in air fryer basket and bake 5 minutes. Set aside.

4 In a separate medium bowl, combine, cream cheese, sour cream, eggs, powdered erythritol, lime zest, lime juice, vanilla, and salt until smooth. Spoon mixture over cooked crust. Cover with aluminum foil.

5 Place springform pan in air fryer basket and cook 14 minutes.

6 Remove aluminum foil and cook an additional 5 minutes at 350°F. Cheesecake will be a little jiggly in the center when done.

7 Refrigerate at least 2 hours to allow to set. Once set, release sides of pan and serve.

PER SERVING

CALORIES: 371	FAT: 36g
PROTEIN: 8g	SODIUM: 253mg
FIBER: 1g	CARBOHYDRATES: 20g
NET CARBOHYDRATES: 5g	SUGAR: 3g

Vanilla Cheesecake with Blackberry Sauce

If you really want a fresh vanilla punch with this cheesecake, use a fresh vanilla bean. However, as a simple substitution you can use 2 teaspoons vanilla extract instead.

- **Hands-On Time:** 10 minutes
- **Cook Time:** 29 minutes

Serves 6

For Cheesecake
1 cup ground walnuts (walnut meal)
3 tablespoons butter, melted
3 tablespoons granular erythritol
12 ounces cream cheese, room temperature
2 tablespoons sour cream
2 large eggs
¼ cup powdered erythritol
Seeds from 1 vanilla bean
⅛ teaspoon salt

For Blackberry Sauce
1½ cups fresh blackberries
2 tablespoons lemon juice
½ cup granular erythritol

1   **To make Cheesecake:** Preheat air fryer at 400°F for 3 minutes.

2   Combine ground walnuts, butter, and granular erythritol in a medium bowl. Press mixture into an ungreased 7" springform pan.

3   Place pan in air fryer basket and bake 5 minutes. Remove from basket and allow to cool at least 30 minutes.

4   Combine cream cheese, sour cream, eggs, powdered erythritol, vanilla bean seeds, and salt in a separate medium bowl. Spoon mixture over cooled crust. Cover with aluminum foil.

5   Place pan back in air fryer basket and cook 14 minutes. Remove aluminum foil and cook an additional 5 minutes at 350°F. Refrigerate at least 2 hours to allow cheesecake to set.

6   **To make Blackberry Sauce:** Place ingredients in a small saucepan and cook over medium heat 5 minutes. Using the back of a spoon, smoosh berries against saucepan while cooking.

7   After berries are popped and sauce has thickened, press through a sieve to filter out seeds. Refrigerate covered until ready to use.

8   Once cheesecake is cooled and set, release sides of pan and serve chilled with blackberry sauce on top.

PER SERVING

CALORIES: 385		FAT: 37g
PROTEIN: 8g		SODIUM: 253mg
FIBER: 3g		CARBOHYDRATES: 39g
NET CARBOHYDRATES: 6g		SUGAR: 4g

Dark Chocolate Satin Custard

Smooth and creamy, this custard will send your taste buds to the heavens whenever that carb craving sneaks your way.

- **Hands-On Time:** 15 minutes
- **Cook Time:** 24 minutes

Serves 4

4 large egg yolks
2 tablespoons powdered erythritol
⅛ teaspoon salt
⅛ teaspoon vanilla extract
1½ cups heavy cream
¾ cup sugar-free dark chocolate chips
1 teaspoon ground cinnamon

1 In a small bowl, whisk together egg yolks, erythritol, salt, and vanilla. Set aside.

2 In a medium saucepan, heat heavy cream over medium-low heat 4 minutes to a low simmer.

3 Whisk a spoonful of heavy cream into egg mixture to temper eggs, then slowly whisk egg mixture into saucepan with remaining heavy cream. Add chocolate chips and cinnamon and continually stir 10 minutes on simmer until chocolate is melted.

4 Remove pan from heat and evenly distribute chocolate mixture among four ungreased custard ramekins.

5 Preheat air fryer at 350°F for 3 minutes.

6 Place two ramekins in air fryer basket. Cook 7 minutes. Transfer ramekins to a cooling rack. Repeat cooking with remaining two ramekins.

7 Allow ramekins to cool 15 minutes, then refrigerate covered at least 2 hours before serving.

PER SERVING

CALORIES: 573	**FAT:** 50g
PROTEIN: 8g	**SODIUM:** 105mg
FIBER: 3g	**CARBOHYDRATES:** 37g
NET CARBOHYDRATES: 6g	**SUGAR:** 3g

Loco Coco Rum Custard

Taste a bite of vacation with this deliciously rich custard. The rum extract gives a little nod to the tropical coconut drink you'd have while sitting poolside.

- **Hands-On Time:** 15 minutes
- **Cook Time:** 19 minutes

Serves 4

4 large egg yolks
¼ cup powdered erythritol
1 teaspoon rum extract
⅛ teaspoon salt
1 (13.5-ounce) can sugar-free coconut cream
¼ cup heavy cream

1 In a small bowl, whisk together egg yolks, erythritol, rum extract, and salt. Set aside.

2 In a medium saucepan, heat coconut cream and heavy cream over medium-low heat 5 minutes to a low simmer.

3 Whisk a spoonful heated cream mixture into egg mixture to temper eggs, then slowly whisk egg mixture into saucepan with remaining heavy cream.

4 Remove pan from heat and evenly distribute mixture among four ungreased custard ramekins.

5 Preheat air fryer at 350°F for 3 minutes.

6 Place two ramekins in air fryer basket. Cook 7 minutes. Transfer to a cooling rack and repeat cooking with remaining two ramekins.

7 Allow ramekins to cool 15 minutes, then refrigerate covered at least 2 hours before serving.

PER SERVING

CALORIES: 297	**FAT:** 26g
PROTEIN: 5g	**SODIUM:** 100mg
FIBER: 0g	**CARBOHYDRATES:** 16g
NET CARBOHYDRATES: 4g	**SUGAR:** 1g

Lemon Curd Palmiers

From the end result, these look impossible to make for a home chef, but in actuality, they are quite simple, with layers of phyllo rolled up with "tart-tastic" lemon curd. Try orange curd for a change of pace.

- **Hands-On Time:** 15 minutes
- **Cook Time:** 24 minutes

Serves 9

3¾ teaspoons granular
    erythritol, divided
1 sheet phyllo dough, thawed
    to room temperature
1 tablespoon butter, melted
⅓ cup lemon curd

HOMEMADE LEMON CURD

Although lemon curd can be purchased jarred in most grocery stores, it can be easily made and is amazingly delicious. Combine 4 large egg yolks and ⅔ cup granular erythritol in a small pot over low heat. Whisk in ⅔ cup fresh lemon juice and 1 teaspoon fresh lemon zest. Slowly whisk in 5 tablespoons unsalted butter, 1 tablespoon at time. Stir continuously until combined and thickened. Strain through a sieve and store covered until ready to use for up to one week.

1. On a flat, clean surface sprinkle 2 teaspoons erythritol over surface. Place phyllo sheet over scattered erythritol. Brush butter over sheet. Sprinkle with remaining erythritol. Flip dough.

2. Evenly spread lemon curd over sheet. Carefully roll one end toward the middle of sheet. Stop at the halfway point. Roll opposite side toward the middle. Refrigerate covered 30 minutes.

3. Slice double log into eighteen equal slices.

4. Preheat air fryer at 350°F for 3 minutes.

5. Place six palmiers in lightly greased air fryer basket. Cook 8 minutes. Repeat with remaining palmiers.

6. Transfer cooked palmiers to a cooling rack. Serve warm or at room temperature.

PER SERVING

CALORIES: 77	FAT: 3g
PROTEIN: 1g	SODIUM: 19mg
FIBER: 0g	CARBOHYDRATES: 13g
NET CARBOHYDRATES: 12g	SUGAR: 11g

Nutty Pumpkin Mug Cake

Enjoy this spiced dessert for one beside the fireplace on a cool autumn night—or wherever and whenever the craving hits! This would be delicious topped with some fresh whipped cream or a scoop of sugar-free ice cream.

- **Hands-On Time: 5 minutes**
- **Cook Time: 25 minutes**

Serves 1

1 large egg
1 tablespoon coconut flour
1 tablespoon almond flour
2 tablespoons heavy whipping cream
2 tablespoons granular erythritol
2 teaspoons pumpkin pie spice
¼ teaspoon maple extract
¼ teaspoon baking powder
2 tablespoons chopped walnuts
⅛ teaspoon salt

1 Preheat air fryer at 300°F for 3 minutes.

2 In a small bowl, whisk egg together with remaining ingredients.

3 Pour batter into a 4″ ramekin greased with cooking spray.

4 Place ramekin in air fryer basket and cook 25 minutes.

5 Remove ramekin from basket and let set 5 minutes. Serve warm.

PER SERVING

CALORIES: 354		**FAT:** 30g	
PROTEIN: 12g		**SODIUM:** 480mg	
FIBER: 5g		**CARBOHYDRATES:** 35g	
NET CARBOHYDRATES: 7g		**SUGAR:** 3g	

WHAT IS PUMPKIN PIE SPICE?
A blend perfect for topping pumpkin pies and other spiced dessert favorites, pumpkin pie spice can be purchased in most stores. However, you can also make your own at home by simply combining the following ingredients: 3 tablespoons ground cinnamon, 2 teaspoons ground ginger, 1½ teaspoons ground nutmeg, 1 teaspoon ground allspice, and 1 teaspoon ground cloves.

Nutty Chocolate Cheesecake

The touch of espresso powder in this recipe enhances the flavor of the chocolate. It's a soon-to-be favorite no one will guess is low-carb!

- **Hands-On Time: 10 minutes**
- **Cook Time: 24 minutes**

Serves 6

1 cup ground pecans (pecan meal)

3 tablespoons butter, melted

3 tablespoons granular erythritol

2 teaspoons instant espresso powder

12 ounces cream cheese, room temperature

2 tablespoons sour cream

2 large eggs

¼ cup unsweetened cocoa

¼ cup powdered erythritol

1 teaspoon vanilla extract

⅛ teaspoon salt

¼ cup mini sugar-free chocolate chips

¼ cup pecan pieces

1 Preheat air fryer at 400°F for 3 minutes.

2 Combine ground pecans, butter, granular erythritol, and espresso powder in a medium bowl. Press mixture into an ungreased 7″ springform pan.

3 Place pan in air fryer basket and bake 5 minutes. Remove from basket and allow to cool for 15 minutes.

4 In a separate medium bowl, combine cream cheese, sour cream, eggs, unsweetened cocoa, powdered erythritol, vanilla, and salt until smooth. Spoon mixture over crust. Cover with aluminum foil.

5 Place springform pan back into air fryer basket and cook 14 minutes.

6 Remove aluminum foil and cook an additional 5 minutes at 350°F.

7 Remove cheesecake from air fryer basket. Garnish with chocolate chips and pecan pieces.

8 Cover cheesecake and refrigerate at least 2 hours to allow it to set. Once set, release sides of pan and serve.

PER SERVING

CALORIES: 458	**FAT:** 43g
PROTEIN: 10g	**SODIUM:** 253mg
FIBER: 3g	**CARBOHYDRATES:** 28g
NET CARBOHYDRATES: 6g	**SUGAR:** 3g

Raspberry Pavlova with Orange Cream

Noted by its crispy exterior and almost marshmallow-like consistency, this beautiful meringue-like dessert was named for Russian ballerina Anna Pavlova. Topped with cream and fresh fruit, this surprisingly low-carb dessert is sure to please.

- **Hands-On Time:** 15 minutes
- **Cook Time:** 90 minutes

Serves 2

For Pavlova
2 large egg whites
¼ teaspoon cream of tartar
½ cup powdered erythritol
½ teaspoon pulp-free orange juice
½ teaspoon vanilla extract

For Topping
⅓ cup heavy whipping cream
1 teaspoon fresh orange juice
¼ teaspoon orange zest
2 tablespoons powdered erythritol
1 cup fresh raspberries

1 Cut a piece of parchment paper to the size of a grill pan. Draw a 6" circle on paper. Flip paper, ink side down, onto grill pan. Set aside.

2 **To make Pavlova:** In a medium metal bowl, beat egg whites with an immersion blender on high. Add cream of tartar, then add erythritol, 1 tablespoon at a time, until stiff peaks form. Add orange juice and vanilla and blend.

3 Preheat air fryer at 225°F for 5 minutes.

4 Spoon or pipe egg whites over parchment paper circle, creating higher edges around perimeter, like a pie crust. There should be a divot in the center.

5 Add grill pan to air fryer and cook 60 minutes.

6 Turn off heat, and let pavlova sit in air fryer an additional 30 minutes.

7 Remove grill pan from air fryer and gently peel off parchment paper from bottom of pavlova. Transfer to a large plate.

8 **To make Topping:** In a small bowl, whisk together whipping cream, orange juice, orange zest, and erythritol until creamy.

9 Fill pavlova with whipped cream and top with raspberries. Serve.

PER SERVING

CALORIES: 191	FAT: 15g
PROTEIN: 6g	SODIUM: 67mg
FIBER: 4g	CARBOHYDRATES: 69g
NET CARBOHYDRATES: 5g	SUGAR: 5g

Chocolate Pavlova with Coffee Crema

Crema is traditionally made with carb-filled buttermilk. Here, the flavor is mimicked with a touch of sour cream.

- **Hands-On Time: 15 minutes**
- **Cook Time: 90 minutes**

Serves 2

For Pavlova
2 large egg whites
¼ teaspoon cream of tartar
½ cup powdered erythritol
1 tablespoon unsweetened cocoa powder
1 teaspoon instant espresso powder
½ teaspoon apple cider vinegar
½ teaspoon vanilla extract

For Topping
¼ cup heavy whipping cream
2 tablespoons powdered erythritol
1 tablespoon sour cream
1 teaspoon instant espresso powder
1 ounce dark chocolate

1 Cut a piece of parchment paper to size of a grill pan. Draw a 6" circle on paper. Flip paper, ink side down, onto grill pan. Set aside.

2 **To make Pavlova:** In a medium metal bowl, beat egg whites with an immersion blender on high. Add cream of tartar, then add erythritol, 1 tablespoon at a time, and blend until stiff peaks form.

3 Fold in cocoa powder and espresso powder. Blend in apple cider vinegar and vanilla.

4 Preheat air fryer at 225°F for 5 minutes.

5 Spoon or pipe egg whites over parchment paper circle, creating higher edges around perimeter, like a pie crust. There should be a divot in the center.

6 Add grill pan to air fryer and cook 60 minutes.

7 Turn off heat, and let pavlova stay in air fryer an additional 30 minutes.

8 Remove grill pan from air fryer and gently peel off parchment paper from bottom of pavlova. Transfer to a large plate.

9 **To make Topping:** Whisk together whipping cream and erythritol in a small bowl. Fold in sour cream and espresso powder.

10 Fill pavlova with whipped cream. Using a vegetable peeler, shave chocolate into curls over pavlova and serve.

PER SERVING

CALORIES: 229	**FAT:** 18g
PROTEIN: 6g	**SODIUM:** 69mg
FIBER: 3g	**CARBOHYDRATES:** 70g
NET CARBOHYDRATES: 8g	**SUGAR:** 5g

Crustless Orange Cheesecake

The citrus in the orange is so fresh and bright, it helps make this a nice summer dessert.

- **Hands-On Time:** 10 minutes
- **Cook Time:** 19 minutes

Serves 8

12 ounces cream cheese, at room temperature

2 tablespoons sour cream

2 large eggs

½ cup granular erythritol

1 tablespoon fresh orange zest

1 tablespoon fresh orange juice

1 teaspoon vanilla extract

⅛ teaspoon salt

1 In a medium bowl, combine cream cheese, sour cream, eggs, erythritol, orange zest, orange juice, vanilla, and salt until smooth. Spoon into an ungreased 7" springform pan. Cover with aluminum foil.

2 Preheat air fryer at 400°F for 3 minutes.

3 Place springform pan into air fryer basket and cook 14 minutes.

4 Reduce air fryer heat to 350°F, remove aluminum foil, and cook an additional 5 minutes.

5 The cheesecake will be a little jiggly in the center. Refrigerate covered a minimum of 2 hours to allow it to set. Release sides from pan and serve.

PER SERVING

CALORIES: 175	FAT: 16g
PROTEIN: 4g	SODIUM: 189mg
FIBER: 0g	CARBOHYDRATES: 15g
NET CARBOHYDRATES: 3g	SUGAR: 2g

Candied Walnuts

These walnuts are a great snack as is, but they also taste delicious as a crunchy addition to yogurt or salad. Try them on the Chopped Steakhouse Salad (see recipe in Chapter 6).

- **Hands-On Time: 5 minutes**
- **Cook Time: 16 minutes**

Serves 6

1 large egg white, beaten
¼ teaspoon vanilla extract
½ cup Swerve brown sugar
¼ teaspoon ground cinnamon
⅛ teaspoon salt
3 cups walnut halves

1 Preheat air fryer at 275°F for 3 minutes.

2 In a medium bowl, whisk egg white together with vanilla, brown sugar, cinnamon, and salt. Add walnuts and toss until well coated.

3 Place walnuts in air fryer basket lightly greased with olive oil. Cook 8 minutes. Stir, then cook an additional 8 minutes.

4 Let cool 10 minutes, then store in an airtight container at room temperature until ready to serve.

PER SERVING

CALORIES: 331	FAT: 33g
PROTEIN: 8g	SODIUM: 59mg
FIBER: 3g	CARBOHYDRATES: 7g
NET CARBOHYDRATES: 4g	SUGAR: 1g

"Grilled" Watermelon

Fruit is a great dessert because of its innate sweetness. And when it is grilled or heated, those natural sugars are enhanced! Enjoy these luscious watermelon cubes after dinner as a light dessert, atop a salad, or even blended into a smoothie.

- **Hands-On Time:** 10 minutes
- **Cook Time:** 4 minutes

Serves 4

2 teaspoons olive oil

2 tablespoons fresh orange juice

1 teaspoon orange zest

1 tablespoon granular erythritol

⅛ teaspoon salt

4 cups 1" watermelon cubes

1 tablespoon chopped fresh mint

1 Preheat air fryer at 375°F for 3 minutes.

2 In a medium bowl, whisk together olive oil, orange juice, orange zest, erythritol, and salt. Toss in watermelon cubes and let marinate 10 minutes.

3 Add watermelon mixture to ungreased air fryer basket. Cook 2 minutes. Toss. Cook an additional 2 minutes.

4 Serve warm or at room temperature, garnished with fresh mint.

PER SERVING

CALORIES: 69	FAT: 2g	
PROTEIN: 1g	SODIUM: 74mg	
FIBER: 1g	CARBOHYDRATES: 15g	
NET CARBOHYDRATES: 12g	SUGAR: 10g	

Blueberries Jubilee

This sweet treat is great served over sugar-free ice cream or topped with whipped cream during those late-night cravings. It's also good in the morning with some Greek yogurt. Or even have it over the Vanilla Cheesecake with Blackberry Sauce (see recipe in this chapter) instead of the blackberry sauce!

- **Hands-On Time:** 10 minutes
- **Cook Time:** 9 minutes

Serves 4

2 tablespoons butter, melted
¼ cup granular erythritol
2 teaspoons cream of tartar
1 tablespoon fresh orange juice
½ teaspoon orange zest
⅛ teaspoon ground cinnamon
⅛ teaspoon salt
2 cups fresh blueberries

1 Preheat air fryer at 350°F for 3 minutes.

2 In a medium bowl, whisk together butter, erythritol, cream of tartar, orange juice, orange zest, cinnamon, and salt. Toss in blueberries. Pour into an ungreased cake barrel.

3 Place cake barrel in air fryer basket. Cook 9 minutes, stirring every 3 minutes.

4 Enjoy warmed or at room temperature.

PER SERVING

CALORIES: 97		FAT: 6g	
PROTEIN: 1g		SODIUM: 75mg	
FIBER: 2g		CARBOHYDRATES: 24g	
NET CARBOHYDRATES: 10g		SUGAR: 7g	

US/Metric Conversion Chart

VOLUME CONVERSIONS

US Volume Measure	Metric Equivalent
⅛ teaspoon	0.5 milliliter
¼ teaspoon	1 milliliter
½ teaspoon	2 milliliters
1 teaspoon	5 milliliters
½ tablespoon	7 milliliters
1 tablespoon (3 teaspoons)	15 milliliters
2 tablespoons (1 fluid ounce)	30 milliliters
¼ cup (4 tablespoons)	60 milliliters
⅓ cup	90 milliliters
½ cup (4 fluid ounces)	125 milliliters
⅔ cup	160 milliliters
¾ cup (6 fluid ounces)	180 milliliters
1 cup (16 tablespoons)	250 milliliters
1 pint (2 cups)	500 milliliters
1 quart (4 cups)	1 liter (about)

WEIGHT CONVERSIONS

US Weight Measure	Metric Equivalent
½ ounce	15 grams
1 ounce	30 grams
2 ounces	60 grams
3 ounces	85 grams
¼ pound (4 ounces)	115 grams
½ pound (8 ounces)	225 grams
¾ pound (12 ounces)	340 grams
1 pound (16 ounces)	454 grams

OVEN TEMPERATURE CONVERSIONS

Degrees Fahrenheit	Degrees Celsius
200 degrees F	95 degrees C
250 degrees F	120 degrees C
275 degrees F	135 degrees C
300 degrees F	150 degrees C
325 degrees F	160 degrees C
350 degrees F	180 degrees C
375 degrees F	190 degrees C
400 degrees F	205 degrees C
425 degrees F	220 degrees C
450 degrees F	230 degrees C

BAKING PAN SIZES

American	Metric
8 x 1½ inch round baking pan	20 x 4 cm cake tin
9 x 1½ inch round baking pan	23 x 3.5 cm cake tin
11 x 7 x 1½ inch baking pan	28 x 18 x 4 cm baking tin
13 x 9 x 2 inch baking pan	30 x 20 x 5 cm baking tin
2 quart rectangular baking dish	30 x 20 x 3 cm baking tin
15 x 10 x 2 inch baking pan	30 x 25 x 2 cm baking tin (Swiss roll tin)
9 inch pie plate	22 x 4 or 23 x 4 cm pie plate
7 or 8 inch springform pan	18 or 20 cm springform or loose bottom cake tin
9 x 5 x 3 inch loaf pan	23 x 13 x 7 cm or 2 lb narrow loaf or pate tin
1½ quart casserole	1.5 liter casserole
2 quart casserole	2 liter casserole

Index

AIR FRY YOUR WAY TO KETO DIET SUCCESS!

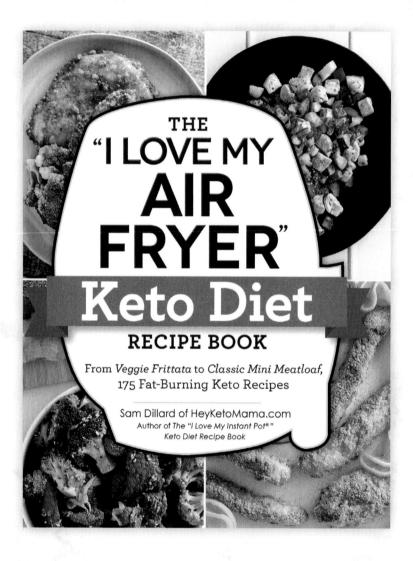

THE
"I LOVE MY
AIR
FRYER"

Keto Diet

RECIPE BOOK

From *Veggie Frittata* to *Classic Mini Meatloaf*,
175 Fat-Burning Keto Recipes

Sam Dillard of HeyKetoMama.com
Author of The *"I Love My Instant Pot®"*
Keto Diet Recipe Book

Pick Up or Download Your Copy Today!

adamsmedia
An Imprint of Simon & Schuster
A CBS COMPANY